FOOTBALL'S
STRANGEST
MATCHES

Other titles in this series:

Cricket's Strangest Matches
Crime's Strangest Cases
Fishing's Strangest Days
Golf's Strangest Rounds
London's Strangest Tales
Motor Racing's Strangest Races
Rugby's Strangest Matches

FOOTBALL'S STRANGEST MATCHES

EXTRAORDINARY BUT *TRUE* STORIES FROM OVER A CENTURY OF FOOTBALL

ANDREW WARD

PORTICO

This edition first published in 2013 by
Batsford
10 Southcombe Street
London
W14 0RA
www.batsford.com

An imprint of Pavilion Books Group Ltd.

ISBN 9781907554087

10 9 8 7 6

A CIP catalogue record for this book is available from the
British Library.

Printed and bound by CPI Group (UK) Ltd, Croydon, CR0 4YY

This book can be ordered direct from the publisher at www.anovabooks.com

Picture credits: p41 © Hulton Archive/Getty Images; p46 © Bob Thomas/Popperfoto/Getty Images; p52 © Fox Photos/Getty Images; p96 © Richard Heathcote/The FA via Getty Images; p142 © Ben Radford/Allsport/Getty Images; p168 © Maeers/Fox Photos/Getty Images.

CONTENTS

THE ONE-MAN TEAM

BURNLEY, DECEMBER 1891

Snow was falling heavily and it was one of the coldest weeks of the year. No one felt much like playing football. Certainly none of the Blackburn Rovers players did; but, being mainly professionals, they came out of the pavilion to take on Burnley.

Conceding three goals in the first 25 minutes did nothing to raise their spirits. Already it was a tetchy game. Two players squared up to each other in a bid to keep warm and settle a quarrel in the cold. When half-time arrived everybody was pleased.

The ten-minute interval passed. Burnley were on the field but there was no sign of Blackburn Rovers. The referee was the notorious J.C. Clegg from Sheffield, a high-ranking FA official and a man to stand no nonsense. Nor did he like waiting in the cold. He warned the teams that he would start in two minutes. In fact he waited four. Even then not all the Rovers players had returned to the pitch.

Soon tempers rose again. The two feuding players came to blows and were sent off. But what followed next was extraordinary. All the Blackburn players except goalkeeper Herby Arthur left the field. The referee, aware that he had done the correct thing by starting the game when there were more than six players, simply carried on. It was Burnley against the opposing goalkeeper.

Herby Arthur was nearing the end of his tremendous career with Blackburn Rovers. He had joined the club as a right-half in 1880, then volunteered to keep goal in the reserve team when a vacancy occurred with no obvious replacement. He played in Rovers' hat trick of FA Cup Final wins in the mid-1880s and became an established England international. Unlike most of the Rovers' players, he remained an amateur.

This was his biggest test. Burnley restarted the game and bore down on his goal.

'Offside,' yelled Herby Arthur.

It was given.

There followed an eternal period of time-wasting. Herby Arthur, with no one to pass the ball to, dallied as long as he could. Eventually the referee gave up and abandoned the game.

Blackburn Rovers later apologized, saying that their players were numb with cold and couldn't continue. Two days later Herby Arthur was given a benefit when Rovers played Sunderland.

THE TRUSTED GOALKEEPER

LONDON, MARCH 1892

When Aston Villa reached the 1892 FA Cup Final, one of the stars of the team was 27-year-old Jimmy Warner, a fine and trusted goalkeeper, one of the oldest players in the team. Five years earlier, Warner had kept goal so magnificently that many said he had won Villa the FA Cup. Now Villa were 7–4 favourites to win the FA Cup again . . . but the bookmakers reckoned without the strangest performance of Jimmy Warner's career.

Villa's short odds for the FA Cup Final were more than justified given their success in the League – they were pressing for the Championship. On the other hand, their Cup Final opponents, West Bromwich Albion, were languishing in the relegation zone.

A week before the Final, Villa flexed their muscles with a 12–2 win against Accrington. Then the team went to Holt Fleet for special training – running exercises, brine-baths at Droitwich and a spell of football practice every afternoon. On the Tuesday, when it snowed, the quick-thinking trainer moved the players into a 70-yard boat-shed and continued the preparations under cover.

Already, during this pre-Cup Final week, Jimmy Warner was being noticed. Not by players, or spectators, or the press, but by Villa committee members, who were monitoring their goalkeeper's activities. It was alleged that Warner would not go through the same training schedule as the other players, and that instead of remaining with his team-mates he 'preferred the company of a certain person to whom the committee objected and who had actually been with him at Holt Fleet against the wish of the committee'.

On Cup Final day, there were about 30,000 people at Kennington Oval, some of them perched precariously on top of the mighty gas-holder. Most knew that on paper Aston Villa should win by a street.

In West Brom's first attack Jasper Geddes sent in a screw shot: 'Warner received it, but the ball seemed to spin out of his hands, and the first goal was scored for the Albion only three minutes from the start.'

It was later described in the press as a 'terrible blunder' but it looked likely to be academic when Villa swarmed to the West Brom end. Jimmy Cowan put a free-kick straight into the West Brom goal-net – nets were being used in a Cup Final for the first time – but as nobody touched the ball it didn't count as a goal, such were the rules of the day.

For 20 minutes Villa used the wind to stay on top, then Jimmy Warner had his second chance to shine: 'Warner partly muffed it, and Nicholls rushed up to send it through the posts.'

After half-time it was 2–0 to West Brom, against the wind, against the odds.

In the 55th minute West Brom's 'Baldy' Reynolds shot from 40 yards. Warner was hopelessly out of position. 3–0 to Albion.

Although Aston Villa dominated the rest of the game, they could not score. Reporters chose words like 'lamentable exhibition' to describe Jimmy Warner's afternoon's work, and Villa fans started their inquests. Attention switched to the Old College public house at Spring Hill, where Warner was the landlord. That evening supporters sought retribution by smashing all the windows in the pub.

A rumour spread. Warner had lost money on a big sporting bet, so the goalkeeper had thrown the FA Cup Final to recoup his money.

Warner vehemently denied this, saying he had bet £18 to £12 against West Brom winning, and an even £1 on them not scoring. Why would he want his business to suffer, his wife blackguarded and a mob threatening his pub? Show us your proof, declared Warner, who promised to give his accusers a good thrashing if necessary.

The next Wednesday, a few days before a vital League game with Sunderland, Warner failed to show for training. The next set of rumours claimed he had taken flight from his pub with a week's takings and a servant girl.

Fielding a deputy goalkeeper, Villa lost at Sunderland, finished fourth in the League and went down 2–0 to West Brom in the semi-final of the Birmingham Cup.

Jimmy Warner had played his last game for Aston Villa. The next season he showed up briefly with Newton Heath (later called Manchester United), no doubt thankful that not every newspaper had castigated him for his bizarre display in the Cup Final. 'Certainly he did fumble a lot with almost every shot he had to negotiate,' wrote one reporter, 'but I incline to the opinion that his backs were outclassed by the Albion forwards, and he, in consequence, was not so fully supported as he was wont to be.'

Perhaps.

THE GAME OF THREE HALVES

SUNDERLAND, SEPTEMBER 1894

On the first day of the 1894–5 soccer season Sunderland were at home to Derby County. The official referee, Mr Kirkham, was late. The game started with a deputy in charge, later named as John Conqueror of Southwick. The two teams played for 45 minutes and then Mr Kirkham arrived. What should he do?

Mr Kirkham made an incredible decision. He offered Derby County, who were losing 3–0, the option of starting again. Naturally they took it. Two more halves followed, and the game became known as 'the game of three halves'.

Derby were captained by England international John Goodall, who lost the toss twice. Derby were forced to kick against a strong gale for the first two halves. But the biggest panic was among the pressmen present at the game. They had already despatched messages all over the country to the effect that Sunderland were winning 3–0 at half-time. Fortunately, Derby obliged by conceding three more goals during the second first half.

Perversely, the decision to start the game de novo probably favoured Sunderland more than Derby. After kicking against the wind for 90 minutes the visiting players were, to say the least, weary. Sunderland scored five more in the third half. The result was recorded as an 8–0 win although Sunderland had scored 11 goals during the three halves. A pattern was set for the season. Sunderland sailed to their third Football League Championship, while Derby were fortunate to hang on to their

First Division status.

The 'game of three halves' assumed a legendary place among the folklore of Derby County players, none more than England-international goalkeeper Jack Robinson, who conceded 11 goals that afternoon. Robinson had previously boasted that he would never concede 10 goals in a game (adding as a joke that he would come out of goal when the opposition reached 9) and his team-mates debated whether the Sunderland game counted as 8 or 11. Robinson explained the débâcle by his failure to eat rice pudding before the match at Sunderland – the only time he missed with his superstition. 'No pudding, no points,' Robinson would tell his team-mates, who would go to great lengths to indulge their temperamental goalkeeper. One day at Burnley, when a hotel waitress announced the rice pudding was 'off', John Goodall went searching for an hour before he came up with a plate of something which would pass for the same dish. Derby County won at Burnley that day, and they played just two halves.

THE FOUR-MINUTE GAME

STOKE, DECEMBER 1894

Referees have discretionary powers to suspend or terminate a game whenever they deem it necessary. In Britain, the reason is usually the weather, although referees are advised to give the matter very careful consideration before yielding to the elements. Otherwise there would be very little soccer played. I know of one Football League game – Grimsby Town against Oldham Athletic in 1909 – where weather conditions twice caused an abandonment. Over a period of seven weeks these two teams met three times and played almost 220 minutes of soccer. Grimsby won 2–0 after trailing by a goal in the second game.

Among the candidates for the shortest-ever game must be the occasion Stoke City entertained Wolverhampton Wanderers in a blinding snowstorm. The weather was so bad that only about 300 or 400 people turned up to watch. Play immediately proved farcical. The referee, Mr Helme, decided to abandon the game after four minutes (some sources say three). The storm soon cleared but the wind persisted, and the conditions were unbearable for spectators and players. For the record, Stoke won the toss.

NOT ONE SHOT AT GOAL

STOKE, APRIL 1898

Modern-day soccer may have its highly developed defensive strategies and across-the-field build-up, but the strangest shot-shy game of all took place more than 90 years ago, when Stoke City and Burnley engineered a goalless draw to save their places in the First Division.

Stoke and Burnley were engaged with two other teams (Newcastle and Blackburn) in a series of test matches to decide promotion and relegation between the two divisions. On the morning of the final round of matches, Stoke and Burnley were joint top of the mini-league. A draw would suit them both, but it didn't suit the 4,000 people who braved torrential rain and strong wind to attend the game at Stoke's Victoria Ground.

It was a fiasco. The goalkeepers hardly touched the ball, passes went to opponents when either team looked well-placed to attack, and, if a forward did by chance find himself in a shooting position he would aim at the corner-flag. Players' kit remained surprisingly clean in the atrocious conditions, and the best chance of a goal was a tame backpass.

The crowd quickly realized what was happening. They booed and jeered, or, for variation, cheered sarcastically. They shouted kind words of advice.

'Come off the field, we're doing more than you!'

'Play the game!'

'Them goal-nets were invented for a reason.'

As the second half progressed, still no goals, still no shots at goal, the crowd on the Boothen Road side of the ground began to make their own entertainment. When the ball was kicked into their small wooden stand, they hung on to it. To their utter disgust another ball appeared. Undaunted, however, they tried again, and again, and again. This small section of the crowd spent most of the second half trying to stop the game by keeping all the footballs. They put one on top of the grandstand and another in the River Trent. Five balls were used altogether, but the game continued to its bitter goalless end.

The crowd's game within a game did lead to the day's best action. A linesman sprinted along the touchline in a bid to catch a ball before it went into the crowd. A perambulating policeman had his eye on the same ball. The linesman collided with the policeman and they lay spreadeagled across the track. The crowd roared, but only with laughter.

The result was never in doubt. Stoke City retained their First Division status and Burnley were promoted from Division Two. Poor Newcastle United, whose players were showing much more effort in defeating Blackburn, finished third in the mini-league, a point behind Stoke and Burnley.

Perhaps one interesting question is how the goalless draw was arranged such that the players trusted one another. Among the participants were experienced Jimmy Ross, who played in five successive test–match series (for Preston, Liverpool and Burnley), and most interestingly, Jack 'Happy Jack' Hillman, the burly and brilliant Burnley goalkeeper whose career was always within a whisker of controversy and comedy.

Hillman, a Devonian by birth, played for Burnley and Everton before a two-season spell with Dundee. During his second season with the Scottish club Hillman was suspended for not trying, which was why he came to Burnley for £130 in time to help them into the First Division. Hillman was then in his late–20s, but much was still to happen to him. He played a game for England, and was twice suspended by the FA – for a season (1900–01) after allegedly bribing Nottingham Forest players to lose to Burnley, and for eight months (1906–07) for receiving illegal payments as a Manchester City player.

Jack Hillman had once won a bet that he could keep goal in a charity match with one hand tied behind his back and not concede a goal. At

Stoke, on that farcical goalless afternoon, he had no need to handle the ball at all. Indeed, he had already bet someone that he would not concede four goals in Burnley's four test matches. He had let in three before the Stoke stroll and there was no chance of a fourth going past him that afternoon.

The Stoke-Burnley game goes down in history on two counts. The authority's disgust at the players' actions led to the curtailing of test matches in favour of automatic promotion and relegation, and, secondly, as far as I am aware, it is the only game without a shot at goal played at the highest levels. There have been games where teams have settled for a result by mutual consent, notably West Germany's 1–0 win over Austria, which enabled both countries to progress to the next group of the 1982 World Cup Finals, and the relegation-escaping 2–2 draw between Coventry and Bristol City in 1977; and there have always been goalless games which tested spectators' patience. When Chelsea met Portsmouth in an end-of-season goalless bore in 1932, the highlight of the game was when the ball burst. 'The ball's packed up,' shouted one spectator. 'Why don't you do the same?'

Any survivors from the Stoke-Burnley pantomime would have sympathized.

COMPLETED – FIFTEEN
WEEKS LATER

SHEFFIELD, NOVEMBER 1898, MARCH 1899

At half-time on a drab November Saturday, Argus-Jud, a Birmingham press-man, bet a Sheffield reporter a cigar and a cognac that the game wouldn't be completed. He won his bet – the game was abandoned ten minutes from time – but the Sheffield man might have felt he had cause for a refund when he heard the Football League's decision. In the 1890s each abandoned game was treated on its merits rather than automatically replayed. For some, the score was allowed to stand. For others, as in the case of this Sheffield Wednesday– Aston Villa game, the game had to be completed at a later date.

The problems started when the match referee, Aaron Scragg, a Crewe fuel agent and FA Councillor, missed his Manchester train connection by ten seconds. He telegraphed to the Sheffield Wednesday offices, but these were some distance from Wednesday's ground. By kick-off time (2.30 pm) no one knew where the referee was.

The game started seven minutes late. A local Football League referee, Fred Bye, took charge until Aaron Scragg arrived at half-time. About 17,000 were present, a good-sized crowd considering Wednesday were on the slide and the weather was dire. It had rained all morning and a keen, piercing wind blew towards the Heeley end. The ground was heavy and the ball fell dead at times. It was also very, very gloomy.

Wednesday took the lead after 20 minutes, Crawshaw's shot hitting the legs of three or four defenders and zigzagging into the net. Aston Villa equalized a minute later. Frank Bedingfield, a late replacement at centre-forward, hooked Smith's centre into the net. It was the only Football League goal Bedingfield would ever score. Three years later he collapsed after playing an FA Cup-tie for Portsmouth and he died of consumption in South Africa not long afterwards.

A goal by Dryburgh gave Wednesday a 2–1 half-time lead. The next goal – Hemmingfield's header giving Wednesday a 3–1 lead – was awarded by match-referee Aaron Scragg, who had finally found his way to the ground. But Scragg's difficulties continued. The pitch was in semi-darkness. Players tried to spot the white shorts or striped shirts that weren't too muddy. Spectators listened for the sounds of players shouting. Some could see the ball only when it was punted above the level of the stands.

There were just over ten minutes left to play when protests by Devey of Aston Villa led to Aaron Scragg consulting a linesman. The game was abandoned and the debate began. Wednesday claimed that their 3–1 lead was the springboard for almost certain victory and they should be awarded the game. Reporters agreed that, from what they could see, Villa looked very unlikely to recover. On the other hand, Villa claimed Wednesday were to blame for arranging such a late kick-off; they should have known November days were gloomy, and therefore the whole match should be replayed.

The Football League, in their wisdom, compromised. They decided the extra ten-and-a-bit minutes should be played on a convenient date. So the game continued . . . 15 weeks later.

One conundrum was how to start the game. Would Aaron Scragg remember where the ball was when he abandoned the game, so that he could drop it from the right place?

A second conundrum was the eligibility of players. Would the same 22 men be forced to resume their places?

A third problem was the likely low attendance. Who would turn out to watch the last ten minutes of a game when the result was cut-and-dried?

The Football League ruled that play would start in the usual manner – tossing a coin for choice of ends and then a place-kick – and that any registered player could take part. In the event, Villa used 13 players and Wednesday 16. No doubt the club secretary needed an abacus to decide how the win bonus would be divided.

Someone had a bright idea to entice the crowd. After the ten-minute farce, the two teams would play a 90-minute friendly (provided the light held good). The proceeds of the friendly would go to Wednesday's Harry Davis, whose benefit match a few weeks before was very badly attended. (On this occasion 3,000 people turned up and Wednesday beat Villa 2–0.)

For 15 weeks Wednesday had desperately needed the two points held in abeyance. Relegation was probable, whereas Villa were favourites for the League Championship. During the infamous 630 seconds of the replay, Wednesday added a further goal to make it a 4–1 victory, but it didn't keep them in the First Division. Villa won the Championship.

This was not the only Football League game to be completed at a later date – Stoke were once ordered to Wolverhampton to play five minutes, and Walsall and Newton Heath completed on a second day – but it proved to be the last. Such was the adverse publicity that the Football League changed its rules over abandoned matches.

In recent years, however, there have been at least two similar events in Spain. A 1989 match between Osasuna and Real Madrid was abandoned after 43 minutes, and the remaining 47 minutes were played just before the end of the season. Osasuna led 1–0 after 43 minutes but Hugo Sanchez equalised three months later. The second example was the 1995 Spanish Cup final between Deportivo La Coruna and Valencia. The first attempt was abandoned after 79 minutes, so the two teams returned two days later and played the remaining 11 minutes.

THE PENALTY-KICKING ELEPHANT

LEICESTER, LATE 1890S

Sanger's Circus was in town. They had an elephant who was unbeaten in penalty-kick competitions. When the circus proprietor issued a challenge to Leicester Fosse professional footballers – no one can beat our elephant – it was a challenge too good to miss. Four Leicester Fosse players accepted and took on the elephant.

For each competition the player and the elephant would take four penalties each. The ball, it must be said, favoured the elephant. It was about six times the size of a normal football.

Three of the four Fosse players lost to the elephant. The last hope was William Keech, who used a crafty penalty-taking technique. Keech feinted to play the ball one side of the elephant, then, as the elephant raised its foot in anticipation, Keech slotted the ball into the other corner. The elephant had met a worthy opponent, but hung on to draw 2–2. A replay was ordered. This time Keech's deceptions were too much for the elephant, who went under 3–2.

So, if you ever get around to picking a team from the animal kingdom to play one of those world teams selected in the back of a football autobiography, please don't forget about the elephant. He may not have much mobility but, with a spot of training, could warrant a place on the substitutes' bench, just in case the game should go to a penalty shoot-out.

SOCCER SICKNESS

LIVERPOOL, JANUARY 1902

The Stoke City management made a serious tactical error before the game at Liverpool – they allowed all the players to eat plaice for lunch. After the half-time interval in the game, only seven Stoke players were fit to resume. The Stoke secretary, Mr Austerberry, was very sympathetic. He was as sick as any of them.

Stoke goalkeeper Dick Roose was in distress before the game started. Roose, a Welsh international, was known as an adventurous goalkeeper whose tactics of wandering all over the field were not curbed until the 1912 change of law. On this day Roose could think only of wandering off the field . . . as quickly as possible. He lasted just ten minutes, by which time Stoke were a goal behind.

'Who wants to go in goal, lads? Come on, someone will have to go in.'

Meredith was the unlucky Stoke player appointed as deputy goalkeeper. For the rest of the first half, during which time he conceded three goals, Meredith made frantic gestures to indicate he would be happier out of goal. His captain, Johnstone, merely flashed back encouraging smiles.

At half-time the busiest man in the dressing-room was Dr Moody, a Stoke director, who examined most of the players and detected signs of lead poisoning. Moody had made his own way to the ground and had therefore escaped the midday meal.

Roose and Ashworth were the most afflicted of the Stoke players, and it was apparent that they would take no further part in the match. Dr Moody also recommended that Watkins and Whitehouse remain in the dressing-room. The only two people in the Stoke party seemingly unaffected were the two trainers, who had passed over the fish at lunch-time.

Dr Moody was left in no doubt about the seriousness of the illnesses. He said later: 'In fact the dressing-room resembled the cabin of a cross-Channel steamer in bad weather, and smelt like it . . . only more so.'

Stoke started the second half with seven players. They played with a goalkeeper – still Meredith – one back, two halves and three forwards. And did quite well too. There was a short spell when Liverpool failed to score.

While people were beginning to debate at what point the game might be abandoned, the two missing forwards, Watkins and Whitehouse, gallantly reappeared against doctor's orders. Goalkeeper Roose, mean-while, who had a pulse-rate of 148 per minute when he left the field, would need a few hours' rest to recover.

In his absence Liverpool scored some soft goals. Not until the sixth went in did Meredith have his wish granted; Clarke took over in goal.

The final total was seven. Not Stoke's favourite number. They had seven fit men, conceded seven goals . . . and lost the next seven games.

FISHERMEN VERSUS FIREMEN

SCARBOROUGH, DECEMBER 1905

The game between the fishermen and engineer deck-hands of Scarborough and district steam trawlers was an annual fixture in the 1900s. It took place on Boxing Day, providing a festive focus for Scarborough people, many of whom gave generously to charity.

The venue was Scarborough's South Sands. Goalposts were sunk in barrels, top hats were worn, and a procession of decorated tramcars paraded through the main streets on the morning of the match. The Rifle Volunteer Band played selections of music as the firemen and fishermen played selections of football. In 1905, the fishermen won 5–3, but the firemen made amends by winning the tug-of-war competition held afterwards.

The 1905 game was particularly important because the remarkably fine weather helped produce record receipts. The proceeds of the game were handed over to two widows. The deceased men were John Lancaster, a well-known Scarborough cobleman, and Robert Thompson, who had been prominent in local footballing circles.

This unusually large gathering of trawlermen also provided the opportunity for other business. Burton Truefitt, a fisherman on a Hartlepool trawler, was presented with a gold watch to commemorate an occasion when he attempted to rescue a colleague at sea, diving into the seas in his oil-skins, returning to the boat to remove clothing and diving again.

The gold watch contained the following inscription: 'Presented to

Burton Truefitt for his heroic attempt to save the life of the late George Whittleton who was drowned at sea, September 23rd 1905, from the steam trawler St Mary.'

UNDER THE SCORCHING SUN

MANCHESTER, SEPTEMBER 1906

At half-time Manchester City players could talk only of the sun, those who could still talk. Outside it was more than 90 degrees fahrenheit in the shade – too hot for sunbathing. There had been no forewarning of the unbearable heat for the newcomers to the City team, especially the Scottish imports, and it was virtually a new-look team because 17 City players and ex-players had recently been suspended by the FA. On the first day of the season, City were sunshocked and shellshocked.

Harry Newbould was the new secretary-manager of Manchester City – several officials had also been suspended after the FA inquiry into financial affairs – and he must have been desolate when he saw the dressing-room scene at half-time. City were 2–0 down to Woolwich Arsenal, three players looked incapable of continuing and it was 60 years before the use of substitutes. Thornley and Grieve were flat on their backs, too ill with sunstroke to do any more work that day. Little Jimmy Conlin, who had sensibly taken the field with a handkerchief tied over his head, had been forced to take refuge in the dressing-room a few minutes before half-time. City were down to eight men.

In Harry Newbould's day, managers were not the strategic conjurors and media magic-men that they are today. Their role was mainly to sign players, pin up team-sheets and ensure the players were all in the right railway carriage.

Newbould was one of the more enterprising of his ilk, and at half-time he might have had some say about tactics on that scorching day.

Translated into more modern managerial hype, the message conveyed to the City players would have been something like this: 'Right, lads, I know it was a bad toss to lose, and it's not the best of conditions, but we'll have the sun on our backs this second half and it'll be the same for them. It's only eleven of them against eight of us. No, Bill, it won't be like this every week in Manchester. Okay, lads, we're two down, and we've only got eight men, but we can go out and take the game to them. I want us to play a 1–3–3 formation this half. That's one full-back, three half-backs and three forwards. And we'll try to catch them offside. Yes, I know you don't know each other very well and only a couple of you have played for City before, but look at it this way, it'll be easier to get to know seven others than ten others. This is a great chance for a good start to the season. And, remember, if you hear the crowd cheering, they're cheering for you, not because they've seen the sun in Manchester.'

Whatever Newbould or anybody else actually said at halftime, it certainly did the trick. Even though City had lost three forwards with sunstroke, they pushed a defender into the forward-line and played a 1–3–3 formation. In the 50th minute Jimmy Conlin returned to the field and the crowd cheered as if they'd seen the sun for the first time.

Taking his position in what was now a 1–3–4 formation, Conlin made a goal for Dorsett, and City, only 2–1 down, were back in the game. But that was as far as it went. Dorsett collapsed soon afterwards, the heat struck down Kelso and Buchan, and City were down to five fit men plus the plucky Conlin.

The referee spoke to his linesmen, but they agreed that there was no just cause for abandoning the game. The Woolwich Arsenal players, meanwhile, were far less affected. They scored two more goals, taking the score to 4–1, but sportingly didn't cash in too much when they faced five fit men in the closing stages of the game.

It took City some time to recover from this setback – two days later they lost 9–1 at Everton – but the new-look team pulled together sufficiently to keep the club in the First Division.

THE CIRCUS GAME

BIRKENHEAD, AUTUMN 1910

There is a particular breed of professional footballer who frowns on people tinkering with the rules of the game. Circus acts belong in the circus, he may say when he discovers a lighthearted experiment at a village fete or local sports. A team once entered a five-a-side competition wearing gorilla suits. Unfortunately one player collapsed with breathing difficulties.

One excellent example of the 'circus game' was that at a village sports near Birkenhead in 1910. A match was arranged between two teams with different handicaps. One team had their arms tied to their sides and their boots and stockings removed. The players of the other team were mounted on stilts, six feet high.

A report in Thomson's Weekly News summarized the play:

'The contest was not so unequal as might have been expected for though those on stilts found it difficult to touch the ball, their antagonists discovered how important a part the arms play in maintaining balance, and when they attempted to run they fell in all directions. In the end the tied arm team won.'

Personally I am not convinced. I am sure I would rather play in a tied arm team than on six-foot stilts, and I wouldn't want to be responsible for anybody who tried to prove me wrong.

THE 'TONYPANDEMONIUM' GAME

TONYPANDY, NOVEMBER 1910

They called it 'Tonypandemonium' when striking South Wales coal-miners rioted and Home Secretary Winston Churchill sent in troops, but the civil unrest had barely died down when the soldiers played the strikers at football.

On Monday 31 October about 12,000 Tonypandy coalminers downed tools. A week later pickets answered a bugle call at 4 am and took to the streets in force. They posted themselves at every street corner and at the entrances to each of the four Cambrian collieries.

The pickets' violence against the collieries included raking the fires from the boilers and stoning the buildings, but that was small-scale compared with the events of Tuesday evening. Shop windows were smashed and the contents were looted.

Troops were called in. A detachment of the North Lancashire Regiment arrived on the Wednesday evening. Less than a week later Major-General Macready reported that order was restored. His report contained a small reference to the evidence of normality: 'A football match between the strikers and the soldiers was played at Tonypandy in which the soldiers were victorious.'

'Pray consult me on any points which cause you embarrassment,' replied Winston Churchill.

The match in question took place on 15 November at the mid-Rhondda ground. The Lancashire Fusiliers, by far the better team, beat mid-Rhondda Athletic 4–1. Each goal was cheered heartily.

DEATH OF A REFEREE

WATTSTOWN, MARCH 1912

The valleys of South Wales have never been an easy territory for soccer referees – heavy, muddy grounds, intense rivalry, fervent supporters and players who usually had their origins in a rugged coal-mining environment. The old chestnut about what's in the game for referees – a small match fee, expenses and a decent funeral – turns sour when we consider the case of William Ernest Williams of Porth, near Pontypridd.

On 15 March 1912 Williams refereed a game at Wattstown, where Aberaman Athletic were the visitors. After the game Williams was brutally attacked while washing himself in the dressing-room. He died as a result of his injuries.

The player responsible, Hansford of Wattstown, was arrested and remanded for trial. He was sentenced to a month's imprisonment for manslaughter.

Several months later, Williams's mother attempted to recover £200 from the South Wales and Monmouthshire FA in an action under the Workmen's Compensation Act. The case, heard at Pontypridd County Court (January 1913), ruled that the referee's contract with the Association was not a contract of service and, anyway, he was paid by the clubs, not the Association. Had the referee been killed during the game, however, it might have been a different story.

BATTLE AT HALF-TIME

BELFAST, SEPTEMBER 1912

Revolvers and knives, sticks and stones, fists and feet. All were used in the battle at Celtic Park. At half-time the Belfast Celtic pitch was a seething mass of struggling men, the police unable to cope.

The riot started suddenly, but many people suspected that it was premeditated. Celtic Park was a Roman Catholic preserve. Linfield, Belfast Celtic's opponents that day, was another Belfast club but with a Protestant following.

Once on the pitch, the crowd split into two factions, one carrying a Union Jack, the other displaying the Belfast Celtic colours of green and white. Thousands were involved in the riot, and the police were swept away in the battle. The din was deafening.

For a time it appeared that people would be killed, but everyone survived the day. The nearby hospital worked overtime to deal with the 100 people who were injured, treating gunshot wounds, fractured skulls and facial injuries.

Hardly anyone was neutral, but if we had to trust a judgement we might rely on the match referee more than others. Mr J.H. Holmes told his story to the newspaper: 'Everything went right to the interval, when, before we could realize it, the pandemonium broke out. We were in the dressing-room at the time, and the officials and players were virtually prisoners. Even when the police reinforcements arrived we were unable to leave, although no attempt was made to molest the club officials or myself. We had a rough time, however, as the departing rioters made a fierce attack on the dressing-room, absolutely wrecking it. The gate money was in an inner room, and even this for a time was in jeopardy, the officials pushing a drawer which contained it against the door as a barricade, which fortunately held good until the rioters passed. During the hottest part of the siege the officials crouched behind, expecting every moment to be struck by stones or overwhelmed by the crowd. We had four policemen laid out in a room at once.'

The riot raged for more than half an hour. There was no hope of restarting the game, which was abandoned at half-time with Linfield leading by a single goal, scored neatly by Smith from McEwen's centre after half an hour's play. It was the only neat thing that happened at Belfast's Celtic Park that afternoon.

THE WAR GAME

NO MAN'S LAND, DECEMBER 1914

The trench warfare of World War One was bloody and slaughterous. British and German soldiers climbed from their respective trenches and charged at each other with murderous abandon. British troops would go over the top with a battle-cry, singing, or, in the case of the East Surrey Regiment on at least one occasion, kicking a football.

Deep down, however, many soldiers knew they were fighting a politicians' war. At times the soldiers at the front had sympathy for each other. From the safety of their trenches they might hold shouted conversations, words travelling across No Man's Land, some of the Germans understanding and speaking English. The conversation could easily turn to football – some Germans had been in England before the war – and the most natural thing for men to do was to challenge each other to a game.

There might have been more contests had footballs always been available. The game most frequently mentioned was that on Christmas Day 1914, when British and German soldiers met in No Man's Land to play their international match. The next day they were fighting again.

ONE-ARMED MEN VERSUS WOMEN

READING, SEPTEMBER 1917

Here was a game strange on four counts. Women played against men; the opposing teams were English and Canadian; the men played with hands behind their backs; and the final score was 8–5.

Perhaps the oddest thing was that men were allowed to play against the women on a Southern League ground. After an early wave of women's soccer in the late 1890s, inspired by the Rational Dress movement and generally believed to be organized by Nettie Honeyball in England and Lady Florence Dixie in Scotland, the FA Council (on 25 August 1902) issued instructions not to permit matches against 'lady teams'. They had a policy of separation – men against men, women against women.

That didn't stop women copying men. In the mid-1900s, six-a-side soccer on roller-skates was introduced for men at Brighton skating-rink, and women soon took up the sport. The goals – 6 ft high and 7 ft wide – were larger than ice-hockey goals, and a regulation-size football containing a pint of water (to keep it from rising) was used. Players were allowed two minutes for skate-repair.

In World War One, with men away in the forces and women in Britain adopting male roles, there was a boom in women's soccer. Although the most lasting development of this period was the Dick-Kerr's factory team in Preston, there were spontaneous outbreaks all over the country, usually based around factories.

The standard picked up enormously. Back in 1895, 'Lady

Correspondent' of the Manchester Guardian had been gently scathing about how well the North and South players knocked the ball about: 'They danced around the ball when they reached it as if uncertain what to do with it, much after the manner of a lapdog which has accidentally laid hold of the cat which he has made an elaborate show of pursuing.' But by the end of World War One the women could play a bit. The Portsmouth Football Mail claimed that Pioneer Ladies captain Ada Anscombe was 'the finest woman player in the country', and alleged that a male team once offered two of their men for her. The FA wouldn't have approved.

The wartime games were usually for charity, and the ladies who played a team of convalescing Canadian soldiers at Elm Park in September 1917 had already handed over £161 to various charities that year. Unfortunately, on this Wednesday afternoon, the conditions were vile. The receipts were probably swallowed up by expenses.

After a band from Bearwood Hospital had played, Surgeon-General Foster, director of the Canadian Medical Services, kicked off. The referee was Colonel Mayus, director of bayonet fighting and physical training. No decisions were disputed.

The women won 8–5 with goals from Miss Barrell (3), Miss Small (2), Miss Wragg (2) and Miss Bentley. It was suspected that the Canadian soldiers were too gallant to win, and in any event there must have been great amusement at the sight of them playing with hands behind their backs. Whether this rule was introduced to balance the sides or to make the women feel safer, I do not know.

SOCCER IN GAS MASKS

VARIOUS LOCATIONS, 1917–18

The Royal Engineers have a rich soccer heritage, so it isn't surprising to discover their participation in gas-mask soccer during World War One.

During the first seven years of the FA Cup (1871–8), the Royal Engineers faced 32 Cup-ties, winning the trophy once and reaching the FA Cup Final on three other occasions. They appeared in the first-ever FA Cup Final (1872) and might have done better than a 1–0 defeat had full-back Lieutenant Cresswell not broken his collarbone after ten minutes.

A Royal Engineers team also won the FA Amateur Cup in 1908, and memories of this success were very clear when World War One broke out. The gas-mask games became a regular part of their training towards the end of the war.

When the whistle went for the kick-off, each player had to take out his gas mask and fit it properly. He wasn't allowed to touch the ball until his mask was properly secured.

During the game the referee would stop the game by whistle and order gas masks to be removed. This time the masks had to be properly put away before players were allowed to touch the ball. The aim, of course, was to familiarize the Royal Engineers with the dexterity needed to use gas masks. The players wore full army uniform during these games, and officers hoped for no serious injuries.

If the notion of soldiers sustaining injuries in soccer games rather than war combat sounds ironic, consider the case of Eddie Mason, a member of the Dragoon Guards for seven years. Mason fought at Marne, Ypres and Aisne and survived the bloodiest war in history with hardly a scratch. Then, in 1919, playing his first game for Hull City, he was carried off in the first few minutes and missed the whole season.

WILFRED MINTER'S GOALSCORING FEAT

DULWICH, NOVEMBER 1922

Never has one man made such a strange goal-scoring impact on a game than Wilfred Minter did that dark Wednesday afternoon in Dulwich. The occasion was an FA Cup replay in the fourth round of the qualifying stage of the competition. In the original game, the previous Saturday, St Albans City and Dulwich Hamlet had drawn 1–1 in controversial circumstances. There was major debate as to whether Redvers Miller's corner-kick had touched any other player before it entered the net – not until 1924 were goals direct from corner-kicks permitted – but referee Rolfe decided it had and St Albans had their late equalizer.

Wilf Minter had been St Albans' outstanding forward in the first game between these two teams of amateurs. He was a local lad, having attended the Hatfield Road school and received football tuition from J. Dickinson, a former St Albans City captain. Minter entered the army when war broke out. While serving overseas he developed his fitness and football talents, and, after demobilization, played for his school old boys' team, helping them to win the 1919–20 Aubrey Cup competition. He joined St Albans City in February 1921 and soon became a goal-scoring phenomenon for club and county. Representative honours followed, but he turned down professional offers to enter his father's business and remain as an amateur with St Albans.

He was to create a record which no professional has ever matched.

The game was played at Champion Hill, Dulwich, where both the home team and St Albans were forced to field deputy goalkeepers after injuries on the Saturday. No doubt this contributed to the afternoon's entertainment. Alf Fearn, a half-back from St Albans Gasworks, was never likely to be a genius at handling corner-kicks and crosses.

Inside 15 minutes Dulwich were a goal ahead. Then Wilf Minter took over. He scored from a crossbar rebound, headed in a Pierce centre and added a third after exchanging passes with H.S. Miller.

After half an hour the score was clear-cut: Dulwich 1 (Kail), St Albans 3 (Minter 3).

During the next half-hour Alf Fearn's lack of goalkeeping experience was exposed. Dulwich scored four times.

After 60 minutes, therefore, the score conveyed a different message: Dulwich Hamlet 5 (Davis 3, Kail 2), St Albans City 3 (Minter 3).

All over? Not quite. When Harold Figg's shot hit a goalpost, Minter followed up to pull back a goal, then he shot two more to give St Albans the lead.

Seventy minutes played, and again the score was transformed: Dulwich Hamlet 5 (Davis 3, Kail 2), St Albans City 6 (Minter 6).

In these earlier days of soccer, people would dispute what was a real hat trick. To conform with the cricketing model – three wickets in three consecutive balls – soccer goals really needed to be three in a row rather than three in a game. But here there was no dispute. Minter had done it twice in one game – three in a row in 12 first-half minutes and three in a row again in 10 second-half minutes. Astonishing.

And there was more to come. Five minutes from the end Dulwich put the ball in the St Albans net. The referee reversed his original decision and gave a goal, much to the dismay of the St Albans players. It meant the scores were level at 6–6 after 90 minutes. Extra-time of 15 minutes each way began in fading light.

After 100 minutes Kail sprinted from the halfway-line and gave Dulwich Hamlet a 7–6 lead. In the gathering gloom, at the other end, Minter was tackled clumsily in the penalty area. Appeals for a penalty were turned down. Too dark for the referee to see, some argued.

With just four minutes to play Redvers Miller took a corner-kick for

St Albans City. This time there was no doubt that someone touched the ball before it hit the net – Wilfred Minter.

Imagine the mood of the man now. Seven goals each and he has scored all his team's goals. The referee is set to blow his whistle as the 120 minutes are just about played. Then the linesman flags and the referee awards a dubious free-kick to Dulwich. Over comes the cross, Davis heads a goal for the London side. The game ends.

Dulwich Hamlet 8 (Davis 4, Kail 3, Nicol), St Albans City 7 (Minter 7).

For an individual to score seven goals is not all that uncommon, but to score all his team's goals including two hat tricks, and for the losing team – that was unique. The next Saturday Wilfred Minter was made captain and the band played 'For he's a jolly good fellow' when he went to the centre of the field for the coin-tossing ritual.

Whether it would have been better to win 1–0 than lose 8–7, we will leave for the modern-day managers to discuss.

STRIKERS AGAINST POLICE

PLYMOUTH, MAY 1926

It seems strange that striking trade-unionists would play the police at soccer on the day of their most intense conflict in history, yet such a match occurred in Plymouth during the 1926 General Strike. A crowd of over 10,000 saw the strikers win by two goals to one. The policemen had their work cut out – on and off the field.

Industrial unrest among northern coal-miners had spread to other industries and services. The effects reached Plymouth later than most towns, but the outcome was devastating. At the end of the first week in May the General Strike was a week old, and the Western Morning News and Mercury was talking of a state bordering on civil war: 'Football is all very well in normal circumstances, and there is no reason why policemen and workmen should not play it. But conditions today are not normal, and a match between policemen and strikers is, at least, strange.'

The events of the Saturday confirmed some people's worst fears. Tramway employers tempted fate by resuming a modified service using volunteers and inspectors to replace the 800 workers who were on strike. Confrontation and chaos was the result. During the morning crowds gathered in the town-centre to prevent tramcars passing.

By 11.30 that Saturday morning there were around 4,000 people doing their best to block the trams. Amidst the jostling a few stones smashed tramcar windows. About 20 or 30 policemen charged the crowd, wielding batons, but it did not prevent the continued harassment of the tramcars. Ironically, this happened just before the soccer match was due to start at Home Park. Once again the police and the strikers were on opposite sides.

The tramway team scored midway through the first half, and a wave of enthusiasm greeted this first – dare I say it? – strike.

Another ironic touch came at half-time, when the music was provided by the tramway band – workers at the very heart of the dispute. When the second-half started, large sections of the crowd followed the band off the pitch and out of the stadium. By the time the strikers scored their second goal, ten minutes from the end, the tramway band was leading a procession of people, four by four, walking along the tramlines to ensure no cars passed. There were more ugly scenes.

Mounted police were called in to deal with a 20,000 crowd in Old Town Street. Three arrests were made, but the tramcar service was withdrawn and the likelihood of pitched battle averted. The next week the strike was called off, leaving the Plymouth strikers with a 100 per cent record on the soccer pitch. That same month games also took place between the Sheffield Police and strikers at Park Colliery.

AMATEURS VERSUS PROFESSIONALS

MANCHESTER, OCTOBER 1926

Take a team of professionals, familiar with each other's play. Include five England internationals. Then pick a team of assorted amateur players. Now play the amateurs against the professionals. Who would win? Yes, the amateurs, of course.

On five occasions, during the 1920s, the Professionals played the Amateurs for the FA Charity Shield. It was soccer's equivalent of the Gentlemen-Players cricket match. There were some who said the professionals played these midweek games with their minds on the week-end Football League programme, but there was certainly pride at stake. In the 1926 Professionals' team there were internationals such as Tom Magee (West Brom), David Jack (Bolton), Bill Rawlings (Southampton), Joe Smith (Bolton) and Fred Tunstall (Sheffield United). The team was selected from the FA party which had toured Canada the previous close-season.

The Professionals scored three goals that afternoon at Maine Road, Manchester, but in between Rawlings's second in the 30th minute and Tunstall's in the last the Amateurs hit half a dozen. Edgar Kail, a full international before the end of the decade, scored the first. Wilfred Minter scored the second. Macey hit the next two, the second from 25 yards, Minter got another, and the sixth was an own-goal. The Amateurs won 6–3.

EXPOSING CHELSEA'S DEFENCE

BLACKPOOL, OCTOBER 1931

Footballers are soft these days, old-time players are fond of telling us. They play in 'carpet slippers', use balloons as footballs and have games postponed if there's a spot of rain on the pitch. An exaggeration, perhaps, but the old-timers could point to plenty of evidence when Chelsea took a fateful trip to the seaside in October, 1931. The game at Blackpool was more a question of how many players would collapse with hypothermia and exposure. At full-time Chelsea were left with six men.

It was a cold, miserable, windy day with ferocious driving rain. Fifteen minutes before kick-off the Bloomfield Road stadium was comparatively deserted. The eventual gathering of 6,000 spectators was about half the usual size. It was a wonder the game started, and Chelsea later complained that the pitch was unfit. Ground staff worked with pitchforks in a futile attempt to clear the water.

Chelsea, missing their famous Scottish International Hughie Gallacher (how glad he must have been), won the toss and sensibly opted to kick with the wind behind them. But conditions soon proved almost impossible. The ball either plopped in mud or squirted over grease. The first chance fell to Jimmy Hampson of Blackpool but he lost the ball in one of the more shallow lakes.

Chelsea found it hopeless to pursue their normal shortpassing game and soon trailed to Wilkinson's 12th-minute goal. Even the referee had difficulty. Mr Jones of Nottingham lost his balance and tumbled to his knees, much to the amusement of the spectators.

In the 31st and 34th minutes Jimmy Hampson scored two freak goals to give Blackpool a 3–0 half-time lead. First the England international centre-forward dribbled round Vic Woodley as the Chelsea goalkeeper lost his footing in the mud. Then Woodley stooped to intercept a cross, fell on both knees, and gasped in amazement as the ball stopped dead in the mud a yard from him. Hampson stepped in, used his foot as a spade and thanked the weather for his second goal.

At half-time came the first sensation. Peter O'Dowd, soon to become England's centre-half, slumped unconscious in the dressing-room. His body temperature had dropped dangerously low. Two other Chelsea players were overcome by the cold. The second half started with only eight in the Chelsea team. Although they were soon restored to ten men, nobody relished the water-polo activities in the Chelsea penalty area. Blackpool's long-ball game was well-suited to the conditions and Hampson completed his hat-trick in the 75th minute.

Immediately after Blackpool's fourth goal, two Chelsea players left the field. The crowd booed and jeered, but it didn't stop another Chelsea player limping off. Soon there were only six left. And, on the same day (31 October), at nearby Blackburn, two of the home side and three Sheffield United players were treated for exposure, while the referee collapsed from the cold. After a 20-minute delay, a linesman completed the game.

At the end of that season (1931–2), Blackpool escaped relegation from the First Division by one point. They were grateful to the day at Bloomfield Road when Chelsea's defence was exposed to the cold.

But even in the 1930s some old-timers were doubtless arguing that it was tougher in their day. There was a famous occasion at Grimsby (in 1912) when six Leicester Fosse players walked off the pitch ten minutes from the end of their 4–0 defeat, and Leicester trainer Harley Thompson was later suspended for enticing them off. And Ernest Needham, Sheffield United's famous international at the turn of the century, recalled a numbing experience at Aston Villa. Writing in his book Association Football, he described it like this: 'The bitterly cold wind and sleet pierced one, numbing muscle and brain. Men on both sides succumbed and were carried away to hot baths and stimulants. I left the field half an hour before the finish of time, and by so doing probably saved my life. Even Foulke was carried in completely exhausted. Several of the Villans did what playing they could in great-coats, and one used an umbrella.'

The legendary Bill 'Fatty' Foulke taking a kick. This giant goalkeeper played his club football primarily for Sheffield United but also spent time with Chelsea and Bradford City in a long and successful career – he even won a cap for England in 1897. Foulke was renowned for his great size (he stood around 6 ft 4 in tall by some estimates) and his immense weight, reaching perhaps 24 stone (150 kg) at the end of his career.

THE FASTEST INDIVIDUAL GOALS

WEST HAM, NOVEMBER 1931

Picture yourself as a supporter of a team which hasn't won for four games. (Some will find this easier than others.) Your centre-forward, Richardson, hasn't been playing well. You would prefer Cookson in Richardson's place at centre-forward. Now you have an away game against a team in London, which means a difficult journey of over 100 miles. However, as the London team is not playing well, you think your side has a chance. You decide to go, but have difficulty finding the ground – your team was promoted to the First Division at the end of last season – and arrive late. You make your way on to the terraces and see someone you know.

'How are we doing?' you ask your mate, knowing that you have missed about ten minutes of the game.

'We're four-nil up,' he replies casually. 'Richardson's got all four and he should have had two more.'

Would you believe him?

Yet, that day in November 1931, you would have had to. W.G. Richardson, the West Bromwich Albion centre-forward, had two good chances in the first five minutes and missed them. Then he scored four times in the next five minutes. It was a remarkable spell of sustained rapid goalscoring, taking advantage of some weak West Ham fullback play and the fact that England international centre-half Jim Barrett was playing out of position at left-half.

The game was virtually over as a contest almost as soon as it had begun. The next goal, scored just after the hour, by Sandford, put West Brom five goals ahead. Jimmy Ruffell headed a reply soon afterwards, and West Ham went down 5–1 on their own ground.

W.G. Richardson's four goals in five minutes is the quickest scoring of four goals on record, a feat equalling that of Jimmy McIntyre of Blackburn Rovers a decade earlier. The difference was that McIntyre's goals came in the second half. Richardson set off one of the quickest starts a soccer game has known.

'AVALANCHE AT ASTON'

ASTON, DECEMBER 1935

Before the away game at bottom-of-the-league Aston Villa, Arsenal centre-forward Ted Drake was worried because he hadn't been scoring too well. He contacted his manager, George Allison, who was in hospital at the time. Allison wrote back indicating how he felt Arsenal could get a 'sackful' of goals against Villa.

On paper it was not an easy fixture. Although Villa were bottom of the First Division, they had spent a lot of money signing new players. Their new team contained six internationals, and it seemed only a matter of time before they put together some good results.

The crowd must have formed the same impression during the first 20 minutes of the game against Arsenal. Villa did most of the attacking but couldn't score. Then Arsenal broke away and Ted Drake scored with his first shot. He also scored with his second, third, fourth, fifth and sixth shots. He hit the crossbar with his seventh, then slammed in his seventh goal with his eighth attempt of the day. Arsenal won 7–1, Palethorpe scoring for Villa shortly after Drake had notched his second hat-trick.

Drake, in fact, scored a hat-trick in each half. His fifth and sixth goals were struck with the supreme confidence of a man who just could not miss the target. Villa had their chances – Palethorpe nearly made it 1–1 with a header and had the ball in the net at 3-0 only to discover Arsenal had been given a free-kick – but the difference between the teams lay in Drake's finishing.

Ted Drake, a £6,000 signing from Southampton, was still in his early

20s. The next year he scored Arsenal's cup-winning goal at Wembley and he helped them to two League Championships. He won five England caps and, as a manager, took Chelsea to the League Championship in 1954–5. Altogether, it was a remarkable career, although he is remembered by many for that sensational day at Villa Park when he earned headlines such as DRAKE'S ARMADA and AVALANCHE AT ASTON.

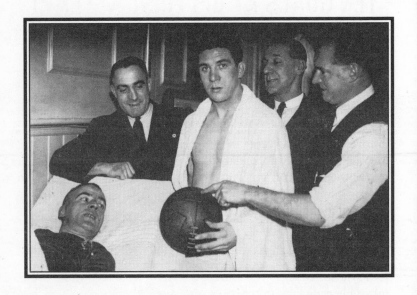

Arsenal centre forward Ted Drake with the match ball after scoring 7 goals for Arsenal as they thrashed Aston Villa 7-1 at Highbury.

TEN GOALS AT HIS FIRST ATTEMPT

LUTON, APRIL 1936

Easter Monday at Kenilworth Road. The home team, Luton Town, preparing for a Third Division (South) game against Bristol Rovers, discovered that they had two centre-forwards on the injury-list. Manager Ned Liddell opted for Joe Payne as a replacement. Payne, a reserve wing-half, had some experience of playing in the forward-line but had never appeared there in the Luton first team. Yet Payne made such an impact that his record may never be beaten.

There was no early hint of what was to come. Payne collected a goal in the 23rd minute and Roberts soon made it 2–0 to Luton, but, five minutes before half-time, the game could have gone either way. Then Joe Payne scored nine in 46 minutes, and no one else scored during this incredible period. With three headers and seven shots, Joe Payne had scored ten goals on his first attempt at centre-forward. Martin scored one in the last minute to make the final score 12–0.

The previous individual scoring record was nine, and Joe Payne's record of ten in a Football League game has held ever since. Payne, a former Derbyshire coal-miner, was 22 years old at the time of his baptism at centre-forward. Two years later, in 1938, he went to Chelsea for £2,000, already an England international. During the war he twice broke an ankle, and never added to the one cap he won against Finland, when he scored two goals. After the war he scored six League goals for West Ham in a spell of nine months – four goals less than he managed in 63 minutes that sensational day at Luton.

TAKING IT AT WALKING PACE

DERBY, MAY 1937

This was the sixth annual walking match between the Crewe and Derby Railway Veterans Associations. Derby held the Cup, having won 2–0 at Crewe in 1936, and were looking to win it two years running (not that the referee would have allowed that).

All the players were over 65 years old. The oldest, Young (Derby) and Betley (Crewe), were both 73. The venue was the Baseball Ground, home of Derby County, and 1,500 spectators turned out on a fine day. The game was one of the most bizarre ever refereed by Arthur Kingscott, who had officiated in two FA Cup Finals, but he had no difficulty keeping up with play, which, at times, reached the frenzied pace of six miles per hour.

Crewe started well on top and looked set for a walkaway victory. By comparison Derby looked pedestrian, which, of course, they were. But once Derby discovered their wing men, the pattern of play changed. Their left-wing pair of Collier and Briddon walked rings round the Crewe right flank, while Radford, only 67, put in some good walks and centres on the Derby right. Radford had the best chance of the match, only the goalkeeper to beat, but shot five yards wide. The crowd groaned. They felt he could have walked the ball in.

The build-up of both teams was slow, naturally, but there was no holding back by the players. One or two of them received minor knocks but were advised by the trainer to 'walk it off'. There were only two things missing. The occasion deserved a walking commentary from a radio station and it also needed a goal.

The game ended 0–0 and both teams shared the Cup, which was filled to the brim and passed round the players at the end. Crewe were optimistic about their chances the next season, when they would be at home. They had a younger team than Derby – average age 68 as against Derby's 69 – and knew the Derby 'lads' would be a year older when they met again.

A MATTER OF CLASS

ETON, DECEMBER 1938

In December 1938 the playing fields of Eton College staged one of the strangest games of Britain's class-conscious society. The Eton College school team took on St Helen's Auckland Social Service team, which was mainly comprised of unemployed coal-miners from the north-east.

Two years previously, Eton College had 'adopted' the St Helen's Social Club centre as part of a goodwill exercise during the days of severe economic depression. Periodically, the boys and staff of the College had travelled to the Durham village of Auckland, involving themselves in the local community activities. As the Auckland Chronicle put it, 'Taking part in the sing-songs, the village teas and suppers, and dances gave them an insight into that quality of warm hospitality which is the quality of the north.'

Now came the opportunity for a trip of a lifetime. The Auckland boys were invited to visit the College at the expense of the Etonians. A game of football was part of the excursion.

The tough, gritty northern lads were expected to give the Eton schoolboys a pretty good game.

At 8 am on Wednesday 14 December, a party of 18 Auckland boys and seven officials set off by motor-coach on the 250-mile journey south. They were cheered loudly by mothers, sisters and sweethearts, who had gathered on a chilly morning to give them a good send-off to the 'far distant land'.

Only six of the party travelling south were in employment. The rest were wondering where their next wage would come from. But for one day the young men from the north-east were given the chance to live like the 1,160 boys at Eton College. On arrival, they were given a hot supper and hotel accommodation. 'They are champion,' one north-easterner said of his southern hosts. 'It's like home from home.'

In the morning the north-east party breakfasted with the schoolboys and attended the Chapel service. Later, after watching work begin in the classrooms, they were taken to see Windsor Castle and St George's Chapel. Then they toured the College buildings and were shown the Tuck Shop – a strategic move, as the football game started shortly afterwards.

The Auckland lads were surprised by the quality of the Eton schoolboys' play. The contest between the polished students and the rough-and-ready unemployed coal-miners was an even one. The result was a 2–2 draw.

The boys ate tea in the College Hall and stayed a second night before travelling home the next day. They agreed that the trip had been grand. One of them, centre-half Makinson, spoke of the best three days of his life.

Top-hatted Etonians socialise with unemployed coal miners from Durham prior to a 'classy' played on 15 December 1938.

'THE MOST FREAKISH, GOALFUL REPRESENTATIVE MATCH OF ALL TIME'

LIVERPOOL, APRIL 1941

'The most freakish, goalful representative match of all time,' wrote L.E.E. of the Liverpool Daily Post. 'It will become one of the talked-of "classics" even if, on this occasion, there was no rabid club partisanship to fire enthusiasms'.

In one respect the reporter was correct – it was the most amazing representative match of all time. In another respect he was sadly wrong – the game between the Football League and a British XI, in aid of the Lord Mayor's Fund, hasn't been mentioned much since that day in April 1941.

Freakishness was quite common during wartime games. Teams were often selected at the last minute because players' availability was in doubt. There are countless examples of double-figure scores being registered against variegated teams containing something like half a dozen assorted professionals, a couple of out-of-position reserves, a cocky local just out of the pub, a spectator who falsely claimed to have played for Aldershot and a trainer playing his first game since Wembley was built.

But this game wasn't like that. The players were all stars. More than half were internationals, nine had played in FA Cup Finals, and there wasn't a laggard amongst them, although there were several decidedly strange incidents.

One of these was the injury of Alf Hobson, the Chester and ex-Liverpool goalkeeper, shortly before half-time. Playing for the Football League – and playing brilliantly – Hobson fell on his head and was carried off with concussion. Tom Galley, the Wolves wing-half, took on the goalkeeper's jersey and also played brilliantly. Billy Liddell of Liverpool joined the game as a substitute.

At half-time, the League led 3–2, but the second half brought eleven goals. Wags suggested that the cricket season had come a month early.

There is only space here to give the order of scoring: Stephenson (1–0 to the League), Nieuwenhuys (1–1), Dorsett (2–1 to the League), Cullis (2–2), Lawton (3–2 to the League), Busby (3–3), Lawton (4–3 to the League), Liddell (5–3), Fagan (5–4), Fagan (5–5), Hanson (6–5 to the League), Lawton (7–5), Stephenson own-goal (7–6), Dorsett (8–6), Stevenson (8–7) and Hanson (9–7 to the Football League).

It may be difficult to believe, but certain reporters at the game commented that it was only the goalkeepers who kept the scores down. And there is a rumour that a dour Lancastrian among the 15,000 crowd turned to his mate at the end of the game: 'Ee, lad, just think. It could easily have finished nowt-nowt.'

FARCE IN THE FOG

LONDON, NOVEMBER 1945

Moscow Dynamo's four-match tour of Britain attracted considerable publicity. The third match of the tour, against Arsenal, was unanimously described as a farce. It was played in a pea-soup fog at White Hart Lane, Tottenham — Arsenal's ground was still requisitioned for war use – and contained many disputes typical of matches between British teams and Continental opposition during that era. Post-match whining shifted between the Russian referee's system and decisions, the fouling, substitutions and, of course, the weather. In one afternoon the Russians were treated to a range of love-hate emotions.

The public became aware of a culture clash at the start of Dynamo's first match of the tour, against Chelsea, when each Russian player presented a bouquet of flowers to his opposite number. They drew that game 3–3, then beat Cardiff City 10–1 to set up an intriguing fixture with Arsenal. George Allison, Arsenal manager, included six guests in his team, the most famous being Stan Matthews and Stan Mortensen (both Blackpool) and Joe Bacuzzi (Fulham).

Fog muffles sound and destroys vision, and London in the 1940s provided regular experience. There is one story about a Charlton Athletic match being abandoned and the players lying in the bath before they realized goalkeeper Sam Bartram was not among them. They found him still in his goalmouth, hopping about, staying alert, thinking his team must be doing all the attacking.

The White Hart Lane farce shouldn't have started. According to the players, visibility was down to a yard or two. The Russian referee encouraged criticism by sticking to the Russian linear system of refereeing rather than the British diagonal system. The two British linesmen were on the same side of the pitch, helped a little by their luminous flags, a novelty in Britain.

Moscow Dynamo scored in the first minute but went 3–1 behind to goals by Ronnie Rooke and Stan Mortensen (2). At half-time Arsenal led 3–2.

Arsenal made a substitution at half-time – goalkeeper Brown for goalkeeper Williams – but later complained that Dynamo had substituted a player in the fog without anybody going off. There were also complaints that players from both sides were committing fouls and then sneaking back into the fog before the referee saw them. Considering visibility was so poor, people had amazing opinions of what was happening elsewhere on the pitch, such as the complaints about the last two Dynamo goals being offside or the shirt-pulling on Stan Matthews. Dynamo won 4–3, and, after the farce was completed, people agreed that the Russians were an excellent team, the best to visit Britain, a passing combination rather than individual dribblers. They went to Glasgow and drew 2–2 with Rangers before leaving.

Similar problems were faced by players during a wartime Edinburgh derby between Hibernian and Heart of Midlothian. Their fog-shrouded match should have been abandoned but it was continued so that German Luftwaffe pilots, listening to the improvised radio commentary, would think it was a clear day over Edinburgh.

THE 203-MINUTE GAME

STOCKPORT, MARCH 1946

No one had yet conceived penalty-kick deciders. When the Division Three North wartime Cup-tie between Stockport County and Doncaster Rovers ended in a draw after extra-time, the two teams were asked to settle the outcome that day. The first team to score would win. But the scores were still level after 203 minutes when the game was abandoned through bad light.

The players were perhaps fortunate that the game didn't take place a month later. Had the clocks been on summer time, play might have lasted until eight o'clock.

The Cup-tie had two legs. The first, at Doncaster, ended in a 2–2 draw. The second, at Stockport, finished with the same 2–2 scoreline. The competition rules dictated extra-time of ten minutes each way. This was played with no scoring. Then the teams played on until the first goal. Referee Baker of Crewe proved a hard taskmaster.

Three times Stockport's Ken Shaw had chances to add to the two goals he had scored in the first 90 minutes. Each time the chance went astray. The game went on and on. Stockport's Les Cocker (later trainer of Leeds United and England) put the ball into the Doncaster net but Mr Baker disallowed the point for an infringement.

There were 13,000 spectators at the game and most stayed until the end. Some went home for their tea and then came back again.

The teams toiled on. The sultry heat took its toll. After 200 minutes Stockport's Rickards tried a shot in the failing light. The ball cannoned off two Doncaster defenders and the goalkeeper. All three Rovers players were left laid out like ninepins. Eventually, after 203 minutes, the referee ended the endurance test. The two teams tossed a coin for choice of ground in the replay. Rovers won the toss and chose their own ground. The following Wednesday they beat Stockport 4–0.

WHEN TWO PLAYERS DIED

ALDERSHOT, APRIL 1948

Soccer can be a lethal game. The most common causes of football death have been serious head injuries (such as those received by the much-lamented Scottish international Jock Thomson), internal injuries (for instance, William Walker of Leith in 1907), pneumonia (e.g. Sam Wynne of Bury in 1927) and infections of wounds, particularly in the earlier years of the game, when internationals like Dunlop and Di Jones died in such circumstances.

Other more unusual fatal incidents have occurred on the field. Thomas Grice of Ashton, Cheshire, fell during a game in 1897 and his belt buckle punctured his stomach. A game in Alicante, Spain, in 1924 was interrupted when the ball brought down a live electric wire and a player who went to remove it was electrocuted. James Beaumont was killed at Walkley, Sheffield, in 1877 when, chasing the ball, he jumped into a quarry.

Such accidents may happen, but clubs can plan emergency proce-dures, medical help and safety precautions to minimize their impact. Sometimes, though, death comes too suddenly. This was the case with the Army Cup Final replay of 1948.

The Cup Finalists were the Royal Armoured Corps (Bovington) and No. 121 Training Regiment of the Royal Artillery (Oswestry). Their first meeting, on Wednesday 14 April, was a 0–0 draw distinguished only by the presence of the King and Queen. The royal schedule was delayed by half an hour because extra-time was played.

The replay also took place at the Command Central Ground in Aldershot. Oswestry scored twice in the first 20 minutes and held their lead into the second half. A storm gathered some distance away. Rain was imminent. Forked lightning flashed its warning. The players took their positions for a throw-in on the opposite side to the grandstand. There was an electric flash of lightning and a simultaneous roar of thunder. The throw-in was never taken.

It was never known what attracted the lightning – some suggested the referee's whistle, others a water-pipe around the track – but the effect was devastating. Eight players and the referee swayed from side to side and then keeled over as though they had been hit on the back of the head. Two players died in the incident – 18-year-old Bertram Boardley, the left-half of the Oswestry team, and his direct opponent, Kenneth Hill of Bovington. The referee, Captain Green, who was on the Football League list, was detained in hospital that evening, and it was suggested that wearing rubber composition footwear might have helped him survive. Two other players and two spectators were also detained in hospital.

For about 30 seconds after the incident no one seemed to have understood what had happened. Then spectators and ambulance men began to move towards the injured. But virtually everyone was in a state of shock, and spectators commented on experiencing a tingling sensation. The game was abandoned and the two teams were given the Army Cup for six months each. The verdict on the dead men was 'death by misadventure, from heart failure, due to an electric shock from lightning'.

A similar event occurred in Birmingham in 1967. A Highgate United player was killed and seven players injured when they were struck by lightning during the FA Amateur Cup tie between Highgate and Enfield. The match was replayed at Villa Park and it was a very emotional occasion for the 32,000 spectators present.

THE INVISIBLE GAME

SOUTHAMPTON, OCTOBER 1950

When Southampton pioneered a floodlit exhibition match against neighbours Bournemouth, about 10,000 people took advantage of the offer of free admission, but they only just got their money's worth. It was a mysterious game that no one could see properly.

The idea emerged from Southampton's summer tour of Brazil, where they played several games under artificial light. The Southampton Supporters' club, on hearing the good reports, invested £600 for a firm called B.A. Corry to install sixteen 1,500-watt arc lamps. Everyone was pleasantly surprised that electricity running costs would be as low as six or seven shillings, so the big question was whether spectators would like it. Here was the big test.

Approaching kick-off time of 6.30 pm, the crowd began to gather and exchange wisecracks.

'Bring on the shadow teams.'

'Come on Wraith Rovers.'

'Pylon the pressure.'

The spectators had to rely on their own entertainment. Although the lights worked well, visibility was destroyed by a familiar British problem – fog. That evening the whole country was enveloped in a thick mist. At London Airport a BEA Viking airliner crashed, killing all 31 people aboard.

At Southampton's ground, the Dell, the fog wasn't too much of a handicap for the players, who could see the ball reasonably clearly, except when it was kicked high in the air, but the referee couldn't see a hand-ball in front of him, and the spectators were literally in the dark. At times visibility slumped to three or four yards and only nearside play could be seen.

The teams played for an hour, changing straight round without a half-time interval. For the spectators it was an eerie experience. In the damp night air, the Bournemouth players, wearing all-white, were a team of apparitions, flitting about like will-o'-the-wisps. From the stand, for all the crowd knew, the players could have been ghosts of the days when footballers wore moustaches and shin-pads outside socks – except for one two-minute period when the fog temporarily lifted and the outcome was theatrical.

There was a rumour that Southampton came close to scoring – Ken Bird pushed Eric Day's shot on to a goalpost – and the consensus was that the game finished without a goal. This was confirmed later by the players.

'Floodlit play needed infra-red glasses,' shrieked the Daily Telegraph headline the next day. Their reporter, Lainson Wood, was dubious about the future prospects of floodlights, saying that no one had made it pay in 20 years of dabbling, and there would always be fog.

Yet several onlookers were impressed.

'There were efforts to introduce floodlight football to this country before the war, but never anything so simple and economical as the installation at the Dell,' wrote Clifford Webb in the Daily Herald.

Another observer – if that is the right term for this fogshrouded night – was Walter Winterbottom, the England team manager. 'This match,' Winterbottom was quoted as saying, 'has proved that even on a foggy night amateur players who cannot train in the daytime can get on to a pitch and have real match practice.'

Here, too, was the crux of Southampton's argument. Their chairman, Penn Barrow, pointed out that the cost of floodlights was far less than the cost of buying players. If they could produce one player from floodlight training it would have paid them.

This game, mysterious though it was to spectators, symbolized a new wave in the floodlighting movement. By the mid-1950s, lights were being used for games as well as for training.

RECORD SCORE

MANCHESTER, AUTUMN 1952

To score more than 20 goals in a game is a phenomenal achievement, one that usually requires a special set of circumstances. The standards for high scoring were set in the last century – Arbroath's 36–0 Scottish Cup win against Bon Accord and Preston North End's 26–0 win against Hyde in the FA Cup – but there have been some good attempts in recent years.

In the inaugural year of the FA Youth Cup (1952–3), Manchester United were drawn away to Nantwich Town. In his book Centenary Dabbers, a history of Nantwich Town, Michael Chatwin tells how Nantwich accepted Matt Busby's offer of £50 to switch the game to the Cliff at Broughton, where the match was played under floodlights. Manchester United loaned Nantwich a set of yellow fluorescent shirts but the Cheshire lads were rarely seen. United were able to call on their Busby Babes, youths like Eddie Colman, Duncan Edwards, David Pegg and Billy Whelan, all of whom lost their lives in the tragic Munich Disaster. They beat Nantwich 23–0 and Edwards scored five from wing-half. But, of course, it was a case of the Nantwich goalkeeper keeping the score down. United were so impressed with George Westwell that they signed him after the game.

Manchester United totally dominated the FA Youth Cup in its early years, winning the trophy five seasons in succession, and this was simply a case of one team being 23 goals better than the other. Some exceptionally high scores, however, are achieved in more suspicious circumstances. The Guinness Book of Records quotes a couple of examples from Yugoslavian football in 1979. Two teams competing with each other for promotion colluded with their respective opponents to improve their goal differences. One won 134–1, the other a mere 88–0.

In the early 1950s an Argentinian team called Wanderers staged a 'sit-down strike' on their pitch, allowing their opponents to win 71–0.

Perhaps the best example of high-scoring was that achieved by two Baden village teams at Frankfurt, West Germany, in 1949. Promised a bottle of schnapps for every goal scored, the teams put on a dazzling exhibition of attacking play. The result – 25 to 24.

SECOND-HALF TRANSFORMATION

LONDON, DECEMBER 1957

It was the Saturday before Christmas. Many of Charlton Athletic's regular supporters had opted for Christmas shopping rather than the home game against Huddersfield Town. Still more did the same after an hour's play. Charlton were losing 5–1 and were down to ten players. It didn't seem worth staying until the end. But let that be a warning. Those who left early missed a most amazing transformation.

Charlton Athletic's home, the Valley, was a huge stadium capable of holding 70,000, and on this pre-Christmas Saturday it looked fairly empty with only 12,500 spectators inside. At half-time Charlton were 2–0 down and not playing well. They had also lost centre-half Derek Ufton, who had dislocated a shoulder, and would have to play with ten men for the last 80 minutes of the game. No substitutes were allowed at that time.

The one man who will be forever associated with Charlton Athletic's stunning transformation that day was Johnny Summers, their tall, stocky outside-left. At half-time he changed his boots, thinking it would be a good time to break in a new pair. After all, Charlton had little chance, and his old pair of boots were falling to pieces.

In the third minute of the second half Summers scored his first goal, but Huddersfield Town popped in three more and led 5–1 after an hour. The visitors, who included future England full-back Ray Wilson and England international wing-half Bill McGarry, looked certainties for two Second Division points, even when John 'Buck' Ryan scored a consolation goal.

Then Johnny Summers scored four goals. In the rearrangements following Ufton's injury, Summers had moved to centre-forward. It was from this position that he scored his goals, all with his unnatural right foot, all wearing his new boots. The remaining spectators were rewarded for their loyalty. They were going berserk and there were still ten minutes to play, Charlton leading 6–5. Then Huddersfield equalized.

The winning goal came with the last shot of the match. Charlton's Fred Lucas fed John Ryan and the big attacker slammed the 11th goal of the second half. Charlton had won 7–6. Moments later, when the final whistle went, the crowd began calling for the players and Johnny Summers in particular. 'We want Summers,' they chanted. At length the players appeared in the directors' box, and were greeted rapturously.

Meanwhile, in the Miller Hospital at Greenwich, the injured Derek Ufton could hardly believe what he was hearing. 7–6? It couldn't have been the game he started off in. It wasn't until team-mate Stuart Leary visited him at the hospital that Ufton could take in the news.

There was a strange sequel less than three weeks later. Charlton Athletic and Huddersfield Town met in an FA Cup third-round replay at the same place, the Valley. A much bigger crowd turned out, expecting a repeat of the goal glut. Charlton won 1–0.

THE TRIPLICATED CUP-TIE

LEEDS, JANUARY 1958

In 1955–6, in the third round of the FA Cup, Leeds United were drawn at home to Cardiff City.

In 1956–7, in the third round of the FA Cup, Leeds United were drawn at home to Cardiff City.

In 1957–8, in the third round of the FA Cup, Leeds United were drawn at home to Cardiff City.

Had the possibility been suggested before the 1955–6 thirdround draw that Leeds would be at home to Cardiff in three successive seasons, a statistician would have calculated the odds at one in two million. Yet something even more unlikely occurred. Let's look at the results.

In 1955–6, Cardiff City won 2–1 at Leeds after a goalless first half.

In 1956-7, Cardiff City won 2–1 at Leeds after a goalless first half.

In January 1958, therefore, there was a sense of déjà vu when 30,374 people visited Elland Road, Leeds, to see the third third-round meeting in successive seasons. Surely Leeds must now gain revenge. The status of the clubs had been reversed. Whereas Cardiff were in the First Division and Leeds in the Second in January 1956, the roles were now the opposite, Leeds promoted, Cardiff relegated. When the teams had met in the First Division, in 1956–7, Leeds had cruised to a 3–0 home victory. It was virtually impossible for three successive 2–1 away wins to occur.

Or was it?

The conditions were icy and precarious. Second Division Cardiff scored first, Alan Harrington scoring from long range in the 20th minute. Bobby Forrest equalized with a header from Wilbur Cush's centre and Leeds took control. Right on half-time, however, came a second Cardiff goal, Cliff Nugent being the scorer. At half-time Cardiff led by the magic, magnetic 2–1 scoreline.

Surely it couldn't happen again – but it did. The referee had the best chance to prevent a 2–1 Cardiff win, when, in the last minute, Wilbur Cush was brought down and Leeds appealed for a penalty. It was not given. Cardiff won 2–1 – three times in a row.

GIANT-KILLING GLORY

WORCESTER, JANUARY 1959

A director of a Fourth Division club once arrived at the stadium on the afternoon of a home tie against attractive First Division opposition. He surveyed the 'icebergs' and ruts at one end of the pitch and the mud and straw at the other and gave his opinion about the obvious postponement. 'Get the referee to play it,' he told the secretary. 'We can beat them on this.'

Ah, the beauty of the British weather in January, the glory of the FA Cup. No book on strange matches would be complete without at least one giant-killing act, where a small club produces an odd result against a big club.

Not all giant-killing, however, is strange. Some teams, like Peterborough United and Swindon Town in the 1960s, were so good at it that people turned up expecting an upset. Some had such good giant-killing years that they almost went the distance. One thinks of Millwall (1937), Port Vale (1954), York City (1955), Norwich City (1959) and Crystal Palace (1976), all of whom reached the semi-final. Certain top clubs create a reputation for being vulnerable. Newcastle United may have won three post-war FA Cup Finals but they have also lost home draws to a galaxy of lower-division teams – Bradford Park Avenue, Rotherham, Scunthorpe, Peterborough, Bedford Town, Carlisle United, Hereford United (in a replay), Wrexham (in a replay), Chester and Exeter City (in a replay). In a year when they did get to Wembley (1974), Newcastle started their Cup run by drawing 1–1 at home to

Hendon. The result was almost predictable.

One of the glamorous features about the FA Cup is that it can create fixtures which are strange (whatever the result): Tooting & Mitcham against Nottingham Forest (1959), Ashington against Aston Villa (1924), Manchester United against Walthamstow Avenue (1953), Lovell's Athletic against Wolverhampton Wanderers (1946), and so on. When a non-League team beats First Division opposition it is front-page news – for instance, Colchester United against Huddersfield (1948), Yeovil against Sunderland (1949), Hereford against Newcastle (1972) and Sutton United against Coventry City (1989).

I have chosen a third-round FA Cup tie on the edge of that pack, one perhaps less remembered, but which, in my opinion, captures the essence of the FA Cup and the vagaries of the British weather. Southern League Worcester City were hosts to Second Division promotion favourites Liverpool, who had lost only two of their last 16 games. Ground conditions for the Saturday of the game were typical Cup-tie conditions. Worcester cleared the snow from the pitch, which then froze. The referee postponed the game.

They tried again the following Thursday. Liverpool had to return tickets they couldn't sell and Worcester City sold them. The crowd was more partisan, the pitch still frozen, the ball erratic in its bounce and not easy to control. In the 10th minute Liverpool full-back John Molyneux tried a back-pass, goalkeeper Tommy Younger did his best to reach it, Worcester's 18-year-old Tommy Skuse skated after it, put the ball in the net and promptly fell over.

Worcester's second goal, in the 82nd minute, was just as unfortunate for the Liverpool defence. Harry Knowles crossed hard from the right, Liverpool centre-half Dick White kicked at the centre and the ball flew over goalkeeper Younger for an own-goal. A minute later Liverpool pulled back a goal, Geoff Twentyman scoring from a penalty.

The last few minutes seemed like hours to Worcester fans. When the final whistle went, the score still 2–1, they swarmed on to the field to congratulate their heroes, throwing hats in the air, engulfing the blue-and-white-shirted players, lifting up goalkeeper Johnny Kirkwood and captain Roy Paul and carrying them from the field. Paul had captained Manchester City when they won the 1956 FA Cup Final.

Worcester City manager Bill Thompson, who had made a few appearances for Portsmouth in the Championship-winning seasons of 1948–9 and 1949–50, could feel proud of his team's gritty performance. The pitch aside, Worcester had played determinedly and won deservedly. That season Worcester set three record attendances for the St George's Lane ground, the first against Millwall in the second round, the last when Sheffield United won 2–0 in the fourth round. Their Cup run should be remembered for the day Worcester City inflicted one of the strangest defeats in Liverpool's history.

THE MISSING FUSES

WATFORD, APRIL 1959

There are several games in which floodlight failure has led to long delays or even abandonments, but perhaps one of the most mysterious was the Watford-Shrewsbury clash close to the end of the 1958–9 season.

Shrewsbury Town were challenging for promotion, occupying fourth place in the new Fourth Division, but they had little to spare and were closely scrutinizing the goal average of fifth-placed Exeter City. Two days after this Watford game, Shrewsbury would face Exeter at home.

Watford, a mid-table team, had little to play for except the end of the season. At half-time they were losing 4–1 to Shrewsbury, having conceded two own-goals on a pitch which was hard, bumpy and of unpredictable bounce.

Halfway through the second half the floodlights suddenly went off. It transpired later that three fuses had been removed. Not a case of sabotage, the police believed, more a case of larceny.

It was an evening game. There was still some natural light, but not enough. Nevertheless, referee Denis Howell started the game again. Meanwhile, club officials tried to do what they could with the floodlights, a bit daunting given the notice on the doors: DANGER, HIGH VOLTAGE ELECTRICITY. Fuse thieves must know what they are doing.

The pitch was virtually in darkness, but the teams did their best to play on. Spectators tried to help by lighting newspapers. Watford's Peter

Walker shot from 35 yards and nobody thought to warn Shrewsbury goalkeeper Russell Crossley that a ball was on its way. It flew past him into the net. Then Colin Whitaker scored one at the other end. Shrewsbury led 5–2, but conditions were impossible. Recognizing the risk of injury, referee Howell abandoned the game after 76 minutes.

Shrewsbury claimed it was floodlight robbery as they needed those two points and five goals for their promotion prospects. The Watford club was fined £100 by the Football League for failing to ensure their floodlights were in order. The game had to be played again. The Football League said it should be played in daylight hours.

When Shrewsbury returned to Watford in the first week in May, having meantime beaten Exeter City by three goals from player-manager Arthur Rowley, they needed a point to guarantee promotion. There was a sense of justice about the result. Shrewsbury beat Watford 4–1, exactly the score when the floodlights failed in the previous abandoned game. They were promoted to Division Three, where they stayed for the next 15 seasons.

'FANTASTIC, INCREDIBLE, AMAZING'

LONDON, OCTOBER 1960

Cliff Mitchell, sports reporter on the Middlesbrough Evening Gazette, ran out of superlatives when describing the Division Two game between Charlton Athletic and Middlesbrough: 'fantastic, incredible, amazing . . . it was rumbustious, dynamic fare and it stirred the blood . . . I can't imagine a more thrilling tussle than this one. It will live for years.'

All the ingredients were right. It was early enough in the season for teams to be carefree, energetic and optimistic. The relentless rain produced a slippery grassy surface which encouraged a fast pace. Both teams were in goalscoring form – Charlton had won 5–3 at Brighton the previous week, Middlesbrough had recently chalked up high-scoring draws at Leeds (4–4) and Plymouth (3–3) – and both clubs had a goal-scoring tradition. Charlton had averaged almost 100 goals a season since they slipped into Division Two in 1957, Middlesbrough had scored over 80 goals in each of their last four seasons.

There were also some special goalscorers in action. Brian Clough, Middlesbrough's England-international centre-forward, maintained a phenomenal strike rate. The player alongside him, Alan Peacock, would also play for England and command a high transfer fee from Leeds United. Charlton had two men, Stuart Leary and Johnny Summers, who would end their careers with over 150 Football League goals.

There were enough incidents in the first 13 minutes to satisfy many crowds for a whole game. Yet there were no goals from this hectic start.

Once the teams started scoring the game went out of control. Eleven goals in 54 minutes: Eddie Werge (1–0 to Charlton after 13), Brian Clough (1–1 after 15), Ron Burbeck (2–1 to Middlesbrough after 17), Dennis Edwards (2–2 after 21), Stuart Leary (3–2 to Charlton after 28), Derek McLean (3–3 after 29), Clough again (4–3 to Middlesbrough after 30), Edwards again (4–4 at half-time), Burbeck (5–4 to Middlesbrough after 49), Clough for his hat-trick (6-4 after 63), Edwards for his hat-trick (6–5 to Middlesbrough after 69 minutes).

The finale was saved for the last minute. Johnny Summers dropped a centre in the Middlesbrough goalmouth. A swarm of muddy players challenged hungrily. Somehow the ball ended in the net without touching anyone. A real old-fashioned goal to end a real old-fashioned game. Six goals each. Fantastic, incredible, amazing.

THE DISALLOWED DOUBLE HAT-TRICK

LUTON, JANUARY 1961

On a day of relentless rain, on a pitch of mainly mud, Denis Law scored six successive goals in 50 minutes to help Manchester City into a 6–2 lead against Luton Town. Unfortunately for Law and Manchester City, the referee abandoned the game after 69 minutes. Luton and Manchester City had to start their fourth-round FA Cup tie again the following Wednesday.

The first meeting had plenty of strange twists. Luton started so well that they were 2–0 ahead after 17 minutes, Alec Ashworth scoring both. Then came Law's spectacular show. The Scottish international showed incredible close-range reactions as he headed and flicked in anything that was in the goal-area, taking advantage of defenders floundering in the mud. One hat-trick was followed by another, but, all the time, there were doubts about whether the pitch was fit. Finally, after 69 minutes, referee Ken Tuck of Chesterfield abandoned the game.

The second attempt started similarly to the first, Luton scoring twice in the first 22 minutes. Denis Law scored for Manchester City just before half-time, but this time there were no hat-tricks to follow. Ashworth's second-half goal sealed a 3–1 victory for Luton, although, overall, Manchester City had scored seven (Law seven) and Luton only five (Ashworth four and Fleming one).

Luton lost 1–0 at Third Division Barnsley in the fifth round.

THE NIGHTMARE DAY-TRIP

BARROW, OCTOBER 1961

Gillingham thought they could travel to Barrow on the day of the game. The journey from the mouth of Kent's River Medway to the tip of the Furness peninsula in Lancashire (as it was then) was over 300 miles. A train leaving London Euston at 9.05 am seemed a safe bet. The team should arrive over an hour before kick-off, which was at 5.15 pm as Barrow had no floodlights.

First came the 35-mile coach trip to Euston. The coach made an early-morning start but ran into heavy traffic. Officials estimated the time-distance equation and grew agitated. The coach arrived at Euston half an hour after the train had left.

The options remaining were not promising. The next train, the 10.25, would arrive one minute after the kick-off. Coach would be far too slow, and cars would be very risky. There was only one possible option – aeroplane. Club officials discovered two suitable scheduled flights – the 10.40 to Manchester and the 11.00 to Newcastle. Both were fully booked.

The next idea was to charter a plane. One was arranged but the company had to fly it from Gatwick to London Airport, where the Gillingham party would be waiting. The cost of the plane was £500 – money in advance.

Gillingham officials also telephoned the Football League. They negotiated a 15-minute delay in kick-off time. The players would be asked to forgo their half-time interval. It was a 5.30 pm kick-off now.

The next problem was the plane's destination. They decided to head for Squire's Gate Airport at Blackpool, about 70 miles from Barrow. This meant arranging another journey. A coach was hired to meet them at Squire's Gate, but, as time slipped by, officials realized a coach would be too slow. Four cars were hired and a police escort arranged for what would be a hectic last leg of the trip.

The charter flight left London Airport at 2.31, having been delayed in a queue of planes. There were less than three hours before the match.

The plane arrived at Squire's Gate at 3.25 pm. Within 20 minutes everybody was in cars. They had a 70-mile journey and 105 minutes.

There were no motorways in the north-west in October 1961. The roads around Morecambe Bay were among the country's worst for a late dash by car through driving rain. They reached Holker Street at 5.30 pm. The players needed to change.

Gillingham, as you can appreciate, were not ideally prepared to play a Fourth Division game. They'd been up early, stuck in traffic on a coach, forced to hang around, shepherded on to a plane (the first time for some), driven rapidly through the countryside and told to change as quickly as they could. By half-time they were five goals down to Barrow.

The problem now was the light. By the 74th minute, when Barrow were leading 6–0, referee Mr Jobling from Morecambe felt it was too dark for football. He allowed an extra couple of minutes under Barrow's training lights – just time for Barrow's seventh goal – but finally abandoned the game shortly after seven o'clock.

The Football League ruled that the 7–0 scoreline should stand as a result. Gillingham's next away game was an even longer trip – Carlisle United. They set off in good time and won 2–1.

ALL IN THE IMAGINATION

FORFAR, FEBRUARY 1963

'It was a great game at Station Park on Saturday although few spectators braved the elements. Three seagulls and a dead sparrow occupied the enclosure, while the only spectator in the stand besides the "Dispatch" reporter was a dispossessed field-mouse.'

That was how the Forfar Dispatch introduced its report of the imaginary game between Forfar Athletic and Stirling Albion during the big-freeze winter of 1962–3. Snow and ice layered the pitches and terraces, matches were postponed en masse and a major casualty was the football pools, until the introduction of a pools panel to fix the results of imaginary games.

The pools companies first disclosed the plan in the third week of January. If there were more than 30 postponements a panel of experts would forecast results of games postponed – home win, away win or draw. (In the 1960s, 0-0 draws counted the same as other draws in pools points.) Doubts about the legality of the scheme were overcome and a panel brought into action. It consisted of Lord Brabazon of Tara (chair) and four ex-international players, Ted Drake, Tom Finney, Tommy Lawton and George Young.

The objectives of the scheme were very clear – to help the pools companies and provide a continuing outlet for the nation's gambling impulses. This was little consolation for non-gambling soccer fans, who had no chance of following a game . . . unless they read the Forfar Dispatch. The reporter took the panel's imaginary result and unearthed an imaginary game which was exciting from the very start.

'Straight from the first blast of the imaginary referee's kidon whistle, Albion swept into the attack. Lawlor, scrambling over a large heap of salt in the Forfar goal-area, got his boot to a loose ball but kicked it high over the bar. Play was held up for five minutes while the luckless inside-right, assisted by his team-mates, searched for his boot in the adjacent field.'

You get the idea?

You are given the result – in this case an away win to Stirling Albion – and you write the match report to fit the result. I'm surprised more reporters don't try it.

The Forfar Dispatch spared us no details. We learn about the first goal – scored by Park while the Forfar goalkeeper had his foot caught in the side-netting – and the three incidents needing the non-existent trainer's magic sponge: Dick shot over the bar and landed heavily when he came down on the other side; Cumming, in agony, pink in the face, clutching his stomach, needed a new piece of elastic for his shorts; and a Forfar forward, through on his own, hit the post, and was carried off with a nasty bump on his forehead.

Reid scored Forfar's equalizer – his colleagues pelted the Stirling goalkeeper with snowballs – and it was 1–1 at the end of the first half, which lasted for 63 minutes as the referee had difficulty defrosting the pea in his whistle.

Both teams scored early in the second half. Soon Forfar led by the odd goal in five, and a very odd goal it was, scored by Dick, who tied his boot-lace to the football-lace and ran 50 yards into the net. An excellent imaginary pass by Stirling's Fish started Stirling's recovery. They went 4–3 ahead but Forfar equalized. Four-four. Time running out. The Forfar Dispatch captured those last tense moments with typical brilliance: 'Forfar officials were already on the phone to London to tell the panel of pools experts that the game was an imaginary draw when, in the dying minutes, Johnstone notched up number five for the visitors, a kid-on away win.'

The reporter added a footnote about the Stirling Albion defender who, on hearing his team had been awarded an away win, went to his manager and asked for his win bonus. 'Surely, I must have told you,' said the quick-thinking manager. 'You were dropped for that game.'

All fiction, perhaps, but this imaginary game had its roots in the reality of a pools-panel away win. From the town that had once provided one of football's most alliterative 5–4 results – Forfar five East Fife four (try saying that in a hurry) – now came the most vivid account of an imaginary 5–4 result. And, just for the record, the pools panel had it correct. When the teams met later in the season Stirling Albion recorded an away win. The score, though, was 2–0.

THE ABANDONED INTERNATIONAL

GLASGOW, MAY 1963

The Scotland-Austria international match at Hampden Park, watched by over 94,000 people, began to simmer in the 16th minute when Davie Wilson scored for Scotland. Austrian players had noticed the linesman's raised flag. Referee Jim Finney waved aside their protests.

After Wilson's second goal, ten minutes later, Austrian centre-forward Nemec was sent off for protesting too much. That left ten Austrians against eleven Scots, and the Scots led 2–0 in goals. By half-time Denis Law added a third goal.

Early in the second half Austria lost the injured Rafreider, who was taken from the field on a stretcher. The teams had agreed to substitute outfield players until half-time and goalkeepers at any time. Rafreider was an outfield player. That left nine Austrians against eleven Scots, and the Scots led 3–0 in goals.

Denis Law scored a fourth Scotland goal, his second of the game. Linhart scored one for Austria. Then came another unsavoury incident. Hof was sent off for a violent tackle. That left eight Austrians against eleven Scots, and the Scots led 4–1 in goals.

After more eruptions referee Finney decided he had had enough. He abandoned the game after 79 minutes, not wanting anyone else to be hurt. After all, it was a 'friendly'.

A PAIR OF BROKEN LEGS

CHESTER, JANUARY 1966

One of soccer's strangest coincidences occurred on New Year's Day 1966 when Chester full-backs Ray Jones and Bryn Jones both broke their left legs in the home game with Aldershot.

There were four players called Jones on the pitch that fateful day – Les was a Chester forward and David was the Aldershot goalkeeper – and, by the 55th minute, when the second injury happened, the others must have been wondering about their destinies.

The first accident occurred in the 21st minute. Bryn Jones tackled Derek Norman as the Aldershot forward carried the ball away. Jones was lying injured when Aldershot's Tony Priscott headed the game's opening goal. But the goal was followed by a bizarre incident – two Aldershot players seemingly fighting each other. Aldershot manager Dave Smith later explained that Norman thought he was being attacked by a Chester player rather than congratulated by a team-mate. Bryn Jones was treated for his leg fracture and taken to hospital.

Chester, with David Read on as substitute, took the initiative and showed why they were chasing promotion from the Fourth Division. Hugh Ryden scored two goals, including a 30-yard shot, and Chester had a 2–1 half-time lead.

Aldershot's Ken Maloy equalized five minutes after halftime. Then came the second tragedy of the day. Ray Jones broke his leg making a tackle, and the next time the two Chester full-backs lined up together was in a hospital ward. On the pitch, Chester, now with ten men, contrived a memorable winning goal for Mick Metcalf.

Despite this 3-2 success, Chester's promotion challenge began to fall away. They were handicapped by the loss of their two regular full-backs for the rest of the season, and were left to digest the peculiarities of the Aldershot game when both full-backs, both called Jones, both broke their left legs.

A TOUCH OF MAYHEM

MONTEVIDEO, NOVEMBER 1967

Celtic, European Cup holders, played Racing Club of Argentina, South America Cup winners, for the championship of the world. Celtic won 1–0 in Glasgow, Racing won 2–1 in Buenos Aires. The play-off was in Uruguay.

Some people suspected there would be trouble. Before the game in Buenos Aires, Celtic goalkeeper Ronnie Simpson was hit on the head by a missile, and John Fallon was hastily substituted. Tension had been building up, and, when the play-off started, referee Rodolfo Perez Oserio from Paraguay soon knew it would be one of his most difficult games. In the 25th minute he called together the two captains and issued a warning.

One man receiving plenty of rough treatment was Celtic winger Jimmy Johnstone, a tiny, jinking player, whose natural game was to take on defenders in tight spaces. In the 37th minute Johnstone was fouled by Rulli, and Celtic players rushed in to protect their winger. Fights broke out and next it was the police's turn to rush in and do some protecting.

After a five-minute delay, Basile (Racing) and Lennox (Celtic) were sent off. The brawl continued with ten a side. By half-time Celtic had conceded 24 fouls and Racing ten.

In the 48th minute, Jimmy Johnstone, fouled yet again, retaliated by hitting Martin. Johnstone was sent off, Celtic were a man short and, eight minutes later, Cardenas scored for Racing, the first goal of the game.

John Hughes was the next to go, sent off for a blatant foul on the Racing goalkeeper. Celtic's chances of saving the game seemed to have completely disappeared, although Racing's Rulli was sent off with four minutes to play. That left eight Celtic players against nine of Racing.

With two minutes to play another free-for-all broke out, and it was a wonder the game was ever finished. The referee implied he had sent off Celtic's Bertie Auld, but the Celtic man was still on the field at the end. By then there was nothing but confusion. And television coverage, claimed by some to be ghoulish, added to the débâcle. Never before had so many players been sent off in a game involving a professional British team.

THE REFEREE'S WINNING GOAL

BARROW, NOVEMBER 1968

Barrow 0 Plymouth Argyle 0. Thirteen minutes to play. Then came a goal to settle this Division Three game, scored by the most unlikely person on the pitch – referee Ivan Robinson.

Barrow won a corner-kick. The ball was cleared out. George McLean shot hard from outside the penalty area and the ball was going well wide. Referee Robinson, perhaps 15 yards from goal, was in the ball's path. He jumped up to avoid the ball but it hit him on the inside of his left foot and flew off at an angle. Plymouth goalkeeper Pat Dunne was completely deceived by the deflection. Having moved to cover McLean's shot, Dunne was stranded as the ball shot past him into the net. Barrow 1 (The Referee) Plymouth 0.

The rules are quite clear. The ball is in play if it rebounds off either the referee or linesmen when they are in the field of play. Ivan Robinson knew that. He pointed meekly to the centre-circle to confirm his goal. Plymouth players looked stunned and shocked.

The incident spurred Plymouth into a frenzied late rally. Barrow hung on to win 1–0 and the referee had to try to avoid congratulatory pats on the back from Barrow supporters as he ran off the field.

Barrow took their unbeaten home run to 18 games and moved into second place in Division Three, probably the highest position they ever reached in the Football League. Diplomatically, they credited the goal to McLean.

Plymouth were left with a long, disconsolate journey home, hardly assuaged by Mr Robinson's subsequent apology.

THE SOCCER WAR

MEXICO CITY, JUNE 1969

At stake was a place in the 1970 World Cup Finals. Two Latin American countries, Honduras and El Salvador, were to play off, home and away, and the winners would meet Haiti to contest one of sixteen places available at Mexico's first World Cup Finals. The outcome of the Honduras-El Salvador confrontation was later dubbed the 'soccer war'.

Antagonism between Honduras and El Salvador had actually been smouldering for ten years or more. The countries had serious internal problems – over-population, poverty and dependence upon simple agricultural economies. By spring 1969 about 300,000 Salvadorans were living in the much larger bordering country of Honduras. Their presence began to be resented, and land-reform laws were introduced to deprive them of farms. On 30 April they were given thirty days to leave their land.

The mood can be gauged by some of the mud that was slung across the border in May. The Honduran Minister of Foreign Affairs linked Colgate toothpaste (made in El Salvador) to an increased incidence of cavities among Honduran children. El Salvador authorities alleged that Glostora haircream (made in Honduras) caused dandruff. By June, the month of the soccer games, tension was running exceedingly high.

Honduras were at home first. The Salvadorans stayed at the Hotel Prado in Tegucigalpa, where they were 'serenaded' all night by whistles, fireworks and shouting. The next day, in the bowl-like stadium at the base of a hill which sported a classical Peace Monument, El Salvador lost

1–0.

A week later came the return game in San Salvador. An El Salvador win would bring a play-off as the competition was on a points rather than goals basis. The Honduras players, not surprisingly, were treated to a reciprocal serenade the night before this return game. Many Hondurans who had travelled to San Salvador caught the hostile mood and decided to watch the game on television instead of attending the Flor Blanca stadium. When they witnessed the stone-throwing and water-bombing they must have been glad to have stayed at home. Furthermore, the game was one-sided. Two goals from Martinez (one a penalty) and one from Acevedo gave El Salvador a 3–0 lead at half-time. There was no second-half scoring but it was now one game each. A play-off was necessary.

Only two Honduran supporters were seriously injured but this was enough to cause outrage in local newspaper columns. The day after the game paramilitary groups in Honduras forcibly evicted Salvadoran peasants from lands they had farmed for years. Tens of thousands of Salvadorans flocked over the border, back to their already over-populated native country.

On 26 June El Salvador broke off diplomatic relations with Honduras. Three days later came the World Cup qualifying play-off. Fortunately, cool heads had suggested a neutral venue. The game was staged at the Aztec Stadium, Mexico City, and about 1,700 Mexican policemen were assigned to duty.

In the circumstances the game was surprisingly peaceful. True, there was one outburst of 'asesinos, asesinos' ('murderers, murderers') from the El Salvador fans, but the fear of feuding among the crowd (about 15,000) proved unfounded, even when the game went into extra-time. The winning goal fell to El Salvador, who recorded a 3–2 victory. Martinez again scored twice.

Early in July Honduran and Salvadoran troops crossed the border. Honduras bragged it had the region's best air force, but, on 14 July, it was El Salvador who made a crucial aerial attack – on the airport at Tegucigalpa. This precipitated the so-called 'soccer war'. The war lasted four days, until economic sanctions by the Organization of American States (OAS) forced El Salvador to withdraw with a psychological victory.

Those people who have studied the war, such as Thomas Anderson in The War of the Dispossessed and Robert Armstrong and Janet Shenk in Salvador: The Face of Revolution, have shown that it was caused by problematic relationships between peasants and landowners, soldiers and civilians, trade-unionists and employers, and was not over anything as 'trivial' as soccer. However, it was certainly one of the strangest political contexts in which a soccer game has occurred.

Nor was that all for the winners, whose progress towards the 1970 World Cup Finals continued to be very odd. After a sound 2–1 win in Haiti, El Salvador might have left reasonably confident. All they required was a draw at home. But Haiti brought along a witch-doctor. He sprinkled some powder on the field, chanted a spell and Haiti were three up at half-time.

The two countries travelled to Kingston, Jamaica, for a closely contested play-off. The game's first goal didn't arrive until extra time, when Martinez scored for El Salvador. Then El Salvador's Argentinian coach Gregorio Bundio took one of the strangest tactical decisions of his career – he punched the witch-doctor and put him out of the game. El Salvador won 1–0.

Bundio had coached El Salvador through ten World Cup qualifying games (including two which went to extra-time), a war and the threat of a witch-doctor. However, he was dismissed from his job before the Mexico Finals, caught up in a dispute between the players and their government. The players felt they were owed money promised for reaching the Finals. The government said the money would have to go towards the costs of the war the players had helped to cause.

In Mexico, El Salvador lost three games – 3–0 to Belgium, 4–0 to Mexico and 2–0 to Russia. They held out for 44 minutes against the hosts, Mexico, and then a disputed goal provoked uproar, threatening to end the match. Eventually the Egyptian referee found an ideal solution – he blew for half-time – and the crowd were left to contemplate the chances of war in the second half.

SOUTH AMERICAN FREE-FOR-ALL

BUENOS AIRES, MARCH 1971

It happened in the closing minutes of a South American (Libertadores) Cup match. Argentinian champions Boca Juniors and Sporting Cristal of Peru were locked at two goals apiece, and 65,000 were watching the contest in Boca's Bombonera ('Chocolate Box') Stadium. Neither side had much chance to qualify from the four-team group, but when Ruben Zune, the Boca Juniors' captain, was tackled and toppled over, he saw red. First he saw his blood. Next he felt his own anger. He attacked his assailant, and then it started.

The scene was what United States ice-hockey followers would call a bench-emptying brawl. Officials, coaches, reserves and almost all the players joined in. Referee Alejandro Otero could do little on his own except stand and observe 19 players commit sending-off offences. He called in the police.

By the end of the fracas three players were injured. Zune's cut would need seven stitches. One Peruvian, Mellan, was carried from the field on a stretcher suffering from a fractured skull. Another, Campos, had a broken nose.

Three players – the two goalkeepers and Boca's Peruvian centre-half Menendez – had steered clear of the rumpus, but the other 19 were arrested by the police. The 16 uninjured players were taken to the police station and given a 30-day jail sentence.

There was real danger of the footballers sewing mailbags in shirts of different stripes with different numbers, but diplomats intervened swiftly. The sentences were suspended. Yet it was six weeks before all the Boca players had served their playing suspensions. Boca, the biggest club in Argentina, had reserves but not of the same standard.

This was another sad episode in the Libertadores Cup, the competition which feeds into the World Club Championship by pitting its winners against the European Cup holders. Originally the Champion Clubs Cup, it had already staged a 3 1/2-hour marathon between Penarol and Santos in 1962 – the Chilean referee twice suspended the game when officials were hit by missiles from the crowd and there were allegations in 1966 that River Plate's two Uruguayans had sold the Argentinian club down its own river. Not to mention a 1970 Nacional-Penarol eruption which was almost on the same scale as the game which saw 19 players sent off. Almost, but not quite.

THE ENDLESS CUP-TIE

ALVECHURCH, OXFORD AND BIRMINGHAM, NOVEMBER 1971

When Alvechurch of the Midland Combination and Oxford City of the Isthmian League played out their final qualifying round FA Cup-tie, people began to joke that the Cup Final might have to be delayed. It took six games and 660 playing minutes to decide the tie. Finally, Bobby Hope's 588th-minute headed goal divided the teams and champagne flowed in both dressing-rooms.

The marathon started and finished on treacherous pitches. The Cup-tie moved from Alvechurch's Lye Meadow (with its corner-to-corner slope) to Aston Villa's Villa Park, calling on the way at Oxford City's White House, Birmingham City's St Andrews and Oxford United's Manor Stadium (where two games were played).

At Alvechurch, the home team led 2–0 but Oxford clawed back into the game to force the first draw. Had Oxford City goalkeeper Peter Harris not dived bravely at the feet of Bobby Hope (not the Scottish international) late in the game, a lot of travelling might have been avoided.

The Cup-tie was chronicled excellently by Oxford Mail reporter Jim Rosenthal, who covered five of the six games. His only mistake was to suggest that Alvechurch might have missed their best chance. 'In this competition,' Rosenthal wrote, 'you only get one bite at the cherry, and Oxford will want to emphasize that point at the White House tomorrow night.'

In fact, Alvechurch had another five bites at the cherry, something neither Rosenthal nor anyone else could have predicted. By the time of the first replay, the two teams knew the winners would play Aldershot (away) in the first round of the FA Cup proper. Aldershot manager Jimmy Melia turned up to watch his future opponents without realizing that he would have four more opportunities to see them play. By the end of the saga Melia might have considered how best to use his time.

The first replay, the most rugged of the six games, had two first-half goals, shared of course. By the end of extra-time the two teams were exhausted, but Alvechurch maintained their season's unbeaten away record.

The next game was in Birmingham – almost a home game for Alvechurch – and the 3,600 crowd was the highest attendance of the six. Having drawn a league game on the Saturday, Oxford City extended their sequence with an equalizer just after half-time of this second replay. But that was the last goal the Cup-tie produced for about 330 minutes.

There was enough action. Another fine save from Harris (after 324 minutes) kept the third match alive, while City's Andy Mitchell cleared from the goal-line (365 minutes) and Tommy Eales twice hit the crossbar (388 minutes and 449 minutes) in the goalless fourth game.

It became an endurance test. Alvechurch midfielder Derek Davis, a car-worker on nights, had to be rested from the fourth game. City's Eric Metcalfe, a schoolteacher, received a hairline fibula fracture in the fifth game. The trainers became experts on cramp.

The Oxford Mail's Bill Beckett, deputizing for Jim Rosenthal at the fourth game, reported that someone in the crowd suggested an annual reunion for those who had thus far watched all four games. Unfortunately, a few minutes after the fifth game (one of three in Oxford), an elderly Alvechurch supporter collapsed and died.

By the sixth game, at Villa Park, there was little new for coaches John Fisher (Oxford City) and Rhys Davies (Alvechurch) to try. The two teams knew each other very well. Fisher was forced to make changes, however, as the Army couldn't release two of his men and two other key players were injured. Then came Bobby Hope's goal in the 18th minute of the sixth game. The winners were Alvechurch.

For the record, the six games were as follows: Sat. 6 Nov. (Alvechurch) Alvechurch 2 (Horne, Allner), Oxford City 2 (McCrae, Metcalfe)

Tues. 9 Nov. (Oxford) Oxford City 1 (Eales) Alvechurch 1 (Allner)

Mon. 15 Nov. (Birmingham) Alvechurch 1 (Alner) Oxford City 1 (Goucher)

Wed. 17 Nov. (Oxford) Alvechurch 0 Oxford City 0

Sat. 20 Nov. (Oxford) Alvechurch 0 Oxford City 0

Mon. 22 Nov. (Villa Park) Alvechurch 1 (Hope) Oxford City 0

(All except the first and last went to extra-time.)

The first round game against Aldershot was delayed, but only by four days. Alvechurch, playing their ninth game in 18 days, went down 4–2 and were out of the competition.

When the draw for the FA Amateur Cup was made a week later you can almost imagine a wag going into the Oxford City dressing-room: 'Heard the draw, lads? Alvechurch away.' Fortunately, it didn't happen.

'We didn't know the Oxford players at the start but we were on first-name terms at the end,' says Graham Alner who played for Alvechurch in all six matches. 'We were turning up as if long-lost mates – the same teams, the same players, the same result. It was a big experience for me. It was character hardening. Tactics went out of the window. We just carried on playing the same way. Before every game, Rhys Davis used to say, "Go out and give it some tonk and bottle." That was his favourite phrase at the time.'

Framed memorabilia of Oxford City's record marathon FA Cup tie against Alvechurch, which had to be played six times.

REFEREE WHO FORGOT THE RULES

LISBON, NOVEMBER 1971

One of the most embarrassing refereeing errors of recent years came when Dutchman van Ravens got the rules wrong during the second leg of a second-round European Cup-winners' Cup-tie between Sporting Lisbon and Glasgow Rangers.

All referees make mistakes occasionally. Such errors usually result from the officials' inability to see everything from every angle and make the correct split-second decision. This gives rise to a spate of jokes and stories about 'blindness' ('I agreed to escort the referee to the railway station,' said the policeman, 'because I always like to take care of the handicapped') and 'bias' ('We were playing against twelve men'). Those familiar with refereeing history are probably aware that many contemporary referees are often compared with the much-respected official in the 1878 FA Cup Final, Mr Segar Bastard.

Most major refereeing howlers occurred in the early days of soccer. There was the referee who ordered off a dumb man for abusive language (the decision was later reversed), the referee who headed a goal (he apologized but had to let the goal stand) and the referee who stood in a dressing-room washbowl and broke it.

In the post-war era a referee at Sunderland in 1954 started the second half before realizing that only one linesman was in place. In front of 43,000 people, his face was as red as the missing flag.

At Wimbledon, in 1983, a referee wrongly awarded Millwall a goal after Wimbledon full-back Wally Downes chipped a direct free-kick over goalkeeper Dave Beasant's head and into his own net. The correct decision here is a corner-kick; the early rule-makers sensibly decided that a team scoring in its own net from a direct free-kick shouldn't be punished more heavily than if it had done so from an indirect free-kick, as the offence being punished was obviously more serious in the first instance.

Refereeing can give rise to all manner of wild questions about soccer oddities and offbeat features of the game. For example, a penalty kick is taken, the ball bursts as it is kicked, the casing flies over the crossbar, the lace spins out and wraps itself around the goalkeeper's neck, hindering him from saving the bladder as it sails into the net – what is the correct decision?

That incident, as far as I am aware, never happened, even in the days when balls had laces. But the events in Lisbon in 1971 showed that one referee had not been tested on the rules of the competition.

Rangers had won the first leg at Ibrox Park 3–2. after being 2–0 ahead at one stage. Now they had a difficult game in Lisbon. Sporting Lisbon twice took the lead. Each time Colin Stein equalized. Then Rangers' Scottish international centrehalf Ron McKinnon fractured a leg, and Sporting took the lead again with 25 minutes to play. Somehow Rangers hung on to take the tie into extra-time.

During this period both teams scored once. Thereupon, referee van Ravens ordered each team to take five penalties to decide the tie. Rangers qualified for some sort of record by missing all five kicks. In fact, Tommy McLean missed twice as the Sporting goalkeeper moved too quickly for the first. Sporting won 3–0 on penalties and were through to the next round. Or were they?'

The Scottish journalists were already scratching their heads in bewilderment. Surely, they thought, away goals count double in the event of a tie. At the end of extra-time Rangers had scored three away goals against Sporting's two in Glasgow.

The referee was wrong. Rangers were indeed the winners. The UEFA officials later reversed the referee's decision and suspended the Dutch referee. The rules were very clear. The provision that away goals counted double in the event of a draw also applied to those scored in extra-time. That gave rise to an even better sporting question: which team missed all its six penalties during a penalty shoot-out and still won the tie?

That season Glasgow Rangers won the European Cup-winners' Cup.

SIXTEEN MINUTES OF DISBELIEF

BIRKENHEAD, MARCH 1972

A strange match creates a crowd atmosphere, a prevailing group mood of anger, laughter, shock or sheer bewilderment, depending on the events concerned. Sometimes, when a match gaily runs completely out of control, spectators turn to neighbours for confirmation of what they are seeing.

That happened to me the night Tranmere Rovers played Walsall. I experienced 16 minutes of disbelief.

It was my second season of supporting Rovers. I had cheered them through their glorious record-breaking season of 1970–1 – no team had ever drawn as many as 22 League games before – and now watched in awe as they blazed a trail towards the Division Three relegation zone. Most Rovers home games were on Friday evenings in those days, the crowd swollen by Liverpool or Everton fans taking a night off from the Anfield Kop or Gladys Street end.

Liverpool fans were particularly enticed in 1971–2, when Tranmere signed Liverpool internationals Ron 'Rowdy' Yeats, soon to become Rovers' manager, and Tommy Lawrence, a goalkeeper affectionately known by the Kop as the 'Fat Cat' or 'Flying Pig'. Lawrence was a roly-poly goalie, small and podgy, deceptively agile, fearless and cumbersome enough to make it very awkward for forwards when they narrowed their shooting angles.

By the time he joined Tranmere, Lawrence was well past his Scottish international peak, slower and heavier, and looking even less like an athlete. I remember one incident when he waddled and grovelled endlessly along the goal-line to collect a stray back-pass near the corner of his penalty area. With no one remotely near him, he stopped the ball with his body, knocked it out of the penalty area, trod on it, picked himself up, dragged the ball back into the penalty area and stood, eventually, clutching his treasure. The crowd had been deathly quiet. Then one spectator spoke clearly and loudly in unsolicited admiration. 'All I saw was a green blur,' he said.

By the end of March 1972, Rovers were still drawing games but not crowds. 'If they played in our backyard I'd draw the curtains,' I remember someone saying at the end of one game. There were just 2,320 present the Monday night Walsall visited.

Occupants of the press-box must have been grateful when news of the attendance reached them in the second half. They could add a comment on Rovers' lowest attendance of the season – in fact it was one of the five lowest in the Division that season – to the meagre notes they already had: drab and goalless . . . both sides failed to control the ball in the wind . . . Tranmere's slump continued . . . Rovers badly missed injured assistant manager Ron Yeats . . . no sign of a goal . . . Chic Brodie showed some neat touches in midfield . . . Rovers failed to take advantage of the gale at their backs in the first half . . . after 62 minutes Adrian Maher came on as substitute for ex-Walsall centre-forward John Manning . . . neither goalkeeper had a save to make . . .

I entertained myself by walking around the terraces, until I was behind Tommy Lawrence's goal, totally alone in that section of the ground. A bitter, biting wind tore through my clothing. In front of me, Lawrence stalked his penalty area to keep warm. I thought about the 20,000 Anfield Kop. Here, at Prenton Park, I was on my own, and it was too cold to stay.

I was on my way home, having just reached the Shed, when the game woke up and went crazy.

A free-kick to Walsall and Mick Evans thunders it noisily against the post and Walsall come again, Chris Jones to Bobby Shinton, whose shot wiggles in the wind with Tommy Lawrence wondering where it went and the game's been given a goal, so Rovers must attack, which they do, Trevor Storton shooting and Stan Jones deflecting the ball up and over

Bob Wesson for an own-goal equalizer, and now the action's back to Tommy Lawrence who knocks down Colin Harrison's shot for Geoff Morris to score another for Walsall and there's nobody on the 'Kop' to see it from close quarters, or to strain their eyes as Wesson makes a great save at the other end and another and another but he can't reach Storton's cross and Maher scores another equalizer so Walsall come straight down and Bobby Shinton topples over Syd Farrimond's legs and Harrison hits the penalty past Lawrence for the third Walsall goal and Rovers have hardly any time left when Maher puts over a corner-kick and Storton lunges and it's Rovers' third equalizer in about ten minutes and the game ends and we can breathe again.

Three-three in 16 minutes. Had it been like that all through the game it would have finished 17 apiece. I have seen games lurch out of control on many other occasions, but never to that extent and never after 74 minutes of tedium. Football, at times, thoroughly rewards the patience of people at places like Prenton Park. That season Tranmere Rovers escaped relegation on goal average.

CROWD POWER

NEWCASTLE, MARCH 1974

Should the Newcastle United–Nottingham Forest FA Cup tie have been abandoned after 55 minutes and the result allowed to stand? If so, Forest would have won 3–1 and gained a place in the semi-final. Instead it took five hours of playing time and many more hours spent in meetings before the outcome was settled. The eventual winners were Newcastle United.

On form, Second Division Forest were given little chance against First Division United, but St James's Park was a likely place for an FA Cup upset. That season Newcastle had twice been held to shock home draws – by non-League Hendon and Fourth Division Scunthorpe United – while two years earlier non-League Hereford United had done the same and then beaten Newcastle at Edgar Street.

Goals by Ian Bowyer and Liam O'Kane gave Forest a 2–1 lead at half-time. Then the eruption came in the 55th minute. David Craig fouled Duncan McKenzie and referee Gordon Kew gave Forest a penalty-kick. Newcastle centre-half Pat Howard argued so much that he was sent off. George Lyall scored the penalty and United, trailing 3–1 on goals and 11–10 down on men, looked a doomed side. A small section of the crowd changed all that.

According to police estimates, between 300 and 500 spectators took part in the pitch invasion. They spilled on to the pitch and charged. Two Forest players were assaulted, so the referee took the players to the dressing-rooms for safety. Twenty-three people were taken to hospital and 103 others treated on the ground. The police made 39 arrests and took eight minutes to clear the pitch.

The teams returned and the game continued, but Forest had lost their initiative. Newcastle surged forward with the bulk of the 54,000 crowd in support. Intimidated, Forest conceded three goals in the last 20 minutes – a penalty by Terry McDermott, a flying header by John Tudor and a volley by Bobby Moncur. One neutral observer said he thought Moncur looked offside but with the crowd in that mood the linesman dared not raise his flag – he would have been lynched.

A special FA commission concluded that the 4–3 Newcastle victory was achieved in a hostile environment. Even though Newcastle had already been drawn against Burnley in the semi-final, the result of their sixth-round game was annulled. The FA ordered the match to be replayed on neutral ground, a decision which infuriated Newcastle officials and players. 'My reaction is one of disgust, but not surprise,' said centre-forward Malcolm MacDonald. 'I half-expected a ridiculous solution, and they came up with one.'

It took two games to reach a decision. The teams drew 0–0 (after extra-time) at Goodison Park on Monday 18 March, and, three days later, at the same venue, Malcolm MacDonald scored the only goal of the game. That season Newcastle reached the FA Cup Final, losing to Liverpool, while people pondered on the long-term implications of that March day at St James's Park. If a partisan crowd was worth a goal start, then a pitch invasion could be worth three.

THE 28-PENALTY SHOOT-OUT

HONG KONG, JUNE 1975

The Asia Cup semi-final between North Korea and Hong Kong finished 2–2 after 90 minutes and 3–3 after extra-time. The ensuing penalty shoot-out had spectators wondering whether it might have been quicker to play another game.

It was an agonizing few hours for North Korea coach Pak Du-ik, best remembered in Britain for the goal that beat Italy in the 1966 World Cup Finals. His team led by two goals in the game against Hong Kong, then looked in danger of losing 3–2 when Hong Kong scored with seven minutes of extra-time remaining. The penalty shoot-out tested the coach's nerve even more.

Hong Kong took the first penalty and scored. North Korea took the second penalty and scored. Hong Kong took the next and missed. North Korea missed their second too, and then the neck-and-neck competition continued.

Each team scored five of their first six. Lai Sun-cheung took Hong Kong's seventh kick. He missed. It was now 'sudden death'. Up stepped Cha Jung-sok to take North Korea's seventh kick. Hong Kong goalkeeper Chu Kwok-kuen saved it.

It was back to stalemate, each team scoring with alternate kicks. Soon, all the players except the goalkeepers had taken kicks, and they had to start over again.

Wu Kwok-hung took Hong Kong's 13th kick and missed.

Pak Jung-hun had the chance to win the game for North Korea but his penalty was saved by Chu Kwok-kuen.

The duel continued.

Hong Kong missed their 14th penalty too, so Kim Jungmm was the next potential match-winner for North Korea. He shot left-footed, low to the goalkeeper's right. Chu Kwok-kuen moved the wrong way and the game was over. North Korea had won the penalty shoot-out 11–10 on the 28th penalty. They were very tired when they beat China in the Asia Cup Final a few days later.

THE ONE-SCORER FOUR-GOAL DRAW

LEICESTER, MARCH 1976

Northern Ireland international Chris Nicholl, later manager of Southampton, played 648 Football League games during his long career with Halifax Town, Luton Town, Aston Villa, Southampton and Grimsby Town. None was more bizarre than Aston Villa's away game at Leicester City in March 1976. which goes down in history for Nicholl's remarkable piece of goalscoring. The tall central defender scored all four goals in a 2–2 draw. Twice he headed own-goals to put Leicester ahead. Twice he equalized with close-range shots.

The game at Leicester was the 18th of 21 away games Aston Villa failed to win that season, their first season back in Division One. They started well enough, but Leicester went ahead after 15 minutes, Nicholl heading Brian Alderson's shot on to a better course for it to find the net. In the 40th minute, however, after Brian Little's header had created confusion in the Leicester penalty area, Nicholl hooked in an equalizer for Villa.

Eight minutes after half-time Chris Nicholl conceded his second own-goal. Leicester's Frank Worthington lobbed the ball into the penalty area and Nicholl, challenging with Bob Lee, sent another fine header past John Burridge. But, once again, he cancelled out his own-goal with one at the other end. Four minutes were left when 'Chico' Hamilton sent over a corner-kick. A scramble in the goalmouth gave Nicholl a chance to put boot on ball, and there was his fourth goal of the game, his second for Villa.

Chris Nicholl's amazing feat of two for each side equalled the 'achievement' of Sam Wynne in a 1923 game for Oldham Athletic against Manchester United. Wynne scored a free-kick and a penalty-kick for Oldham and two own-goals for Manchester United. Oldham won 3–2. But, in Nicholl's case, all his goals came from open play and they were the only goals of the game.

Also, there were a couple of strange indicators from the previous week. Chris Nicholl had scored an own-goal a week before, diverting a shot from Tottenham Hotspur's Ralph Coates past John Burridge. And, on the same day, Leicester had beaten Middlesbrough, the only goal of the game being an own-goal by tall Middlesbrough central defender Stuart Boam.

One of the strangest things about Nicholl's performance was his two goals for Villa. His goals usually came from his head, but here he was scoring with his feet. It was surprising that Villa never used him as an out-and-out attacker. After all, that day at Leicester he demonstrated that he had the one thing that all natural goalscorers possess – a beautiful sense of balance.

THE GAME THAT NEVER WAS

LEATHERHEAD, FEBRUARY 1978

Leatherhead were drawn at home to Dartford in the second round of the FA Trophy. Conditions were not good, but match referee Vickers of Essex declared the pitch fit after an inspection an hour and a half before kick-off. Dartford never turned up.

The Leatherhead players waited, the crowd at Fetcham Grove waited, even the Dartford directors who had travelled under their own steam waited. There was no sign of the Dartford team coach.

There were four differing accounts of why the Dartford coach-driver was told to turn round at Croydon, which was over halfway of a journey of less than 30 miles. Certainly someone made a telephone call from Croydon. One account says a young girl answered and told them the game was postponed. Another says it was the secretary who confirmed the match was off. A third account suggests Dartford were the victims of a hoax. A fourth guess might be that someone dialled the wrong number. If a stranger phoned your house at Saturday lunchtime and came straight to the point – 'Is the game on, Leatherhead?' – you probably wouldn't be stuck for a negative answer.

So, while Dartford players were at home watching the rugby on television, Leatherhead players were put through a stiff training session. Although people at the ground felt Dartford were to blame, no one was fined over the incident. Dartford were allowed to replay the fixture without punishment. On the following Thursday Leatherhead won 5–1, Chris Kelly scoring two goals.

The morals of the tale are to ensure that telephones are staffed responsibly at key times and to seek confirmation of any news received. These points can be made more forcibly by reference to a cunning piece of corruption which took place in 1904. Before an important game between Bristol East and Warmley, the Bristol East goalkeeper received a telegram from the Bristol East secretary saying the match would not take place. Warmley were delighted when Bristol East were forced to scratch around at the last minute for a replacement goalkeeper. When it was later learned that the telegram had been sent by Warmley officials, the Football Association handed out three suspensions.

WARRING TEAM-MATES

LONDON, JANUARY 1979

There is a clear statement contained in the twelfth of soccer's 17 laws: a player shall be sent off the field of play if, in the opinion of the referee, he is guilty of violent conduct or serious foul play.

This statement does not specify that the violent conduct must be towards an opponent for it to warrant a sending-off punishment. The violence could be directed at a team-mate, although that is extremely rare.

There were five minutes to play in the game at the Valley Stadium. Charlton Athletic and Maidstone United were drawing 1–1 in their FA Cup third-round game. Mike Flanagan, scorer of Charlton's equalizer a few minutes before, played the ball through. Derek Hales, Flanagan's co-striker, was given offside. The bearded Hales was not pleased.

Hales made it clear that he wanted the ball played earlier. Flanagan said something to the effect that he had been doing that all season and it hadn't come to much. Hales and Flanagan swore at each other. Then they started fighting. Referee Brian Martin had no option but to send off both players.

Everyone was stunned. It was outside most people's experience. There had been a similar incident in Scotland, when two Stranraer players came to blows in 1975, but they had escaped with cautions and very few heard about it. Now Charlton had to complete the game with nine men. They held on and won a replay.

The following week over 10,000 spectators attended the replay in the hope of seeing an upset. The Southern League Premier Division team, unbeaten in 14 games, now had ground advantage, and Second Division Charlton would be without Hales and Flanagan, suspended after their sending-off incident. What they saw was a match which was definitely a bit strange.

Goals by David Campbell and Martyn Robinson gave Charlton a healthy 2–0 lead. Glen Coupland pulled one back with four minutes to play. Then the floodlights went out.

The lights had overheated. There was a 17-minute time-out before they were restored and play resumed. The final two or three minutes were played out with no more score. Maidstone, who had beaten Exeter City in the previous round, were knocked out of the FA Cup for that season. Charlton went out at Bristol Rovers in the fourth round, the only game Mike Flanagan played during the last four months of the season.

Hales and Flanagan both received punishments from Charlton, and Flanagan was later suspended by the club when he implied that the personal difficulties with Hales would prevent him playing. Six months later, after much inactivity, Flanagan moved to Crystal Palace. From there he moved to Queen's Park Rangers. In January 1984, however, Flanagan signed once more for Charlton Athletic, where, for nearly a year he resumed his successful striking partnership with Derek Hales.

THE FALKLAND ISLANDS GAMES

SOUTH GEORGIA, THROUGH THE 1970S

Sometimes the setting is enough to provide a strange game. In 1920–1, at Fishguard on the Welsh coast, players had to swim out to sea to rescue a football before a game could continue. Other games are played next to rivers, with trees overhanging the pitch or with quarries behind one goal. All seem odd when encountered for the first time.

In the 1970s, the British Antarctic Survey team regularly played soccer matches against the crews of ships using the water facilities of the whaling station on South Georgia in the Falkland Isles. Their team was selected from about 20 men on base. They changed in an old cinema and drove to the whaling-station pitch in a tractor and trailer. The pitch, like all unusual settings, was worth a start in goals to the home team. It was cut into the base of a mountain, and local grass covered the stone surface, which, obviously, wasn't the best surface for sliding tackles or the longevity of football boots and footballs. There were no pitch markings but natural boundaries. Three sides were marked by obvious banks. The fourth fell away so that the ball could roll into a stream, a dyke or down drainage holes. Mount Hodges (2,000 ft) acted as a huge spion kop.

A LEGAL PRECEDENT

LEAMINGTON SPA, JANUARY 1980

A foul tackle by Gurdever Basi of Khalsa Football Club broke the right leg of James Condon of Whittle Wanderers in a local league game. Condon was off work for nine months. More than a year after the game he issued a writ suing Basi for damages. He alleged negligence and deliberate and wrongful assault. He won his case.

The case was heard by Judge Wootton at Warwick County Court in March 1984. Basi was found guilty of negligence and Condon was awarded damages of £4,900 plus interest and costs. Basi's appeal was dismissed by Judge Donaldson in May 1985.

For a description of the incident we can rely on the referee's report of the Whittle Wanderers–Khalsa game. An experienced Class 1 official, he wrote this: 'After 62 minutes of play of the above game, a player from Whittle Wanderers received possession of the ball some 15 yards inside Khalsa Football Club's half of the field of play. This Whittle Wanderers player upon realizing that he was about to be challenged for the ball by an opponent pushed the ball away. As he did so, the opponent (the defendant) challenged, by sliding in from a distance of three or four yards. The slide tackle came late, and was made in a reckless and dangerous manner, by lunging with his boot studs showing about a foot to 18 inches from the ground. The result of this tackle was that (the plaintiff) sustained a broken right leg. In my opinion, the tackle constituted serious foul play and I sent (the defendant) from the field of play.'

Such cases depend on determining what is meant by 'care'. Footballers have a duty to take all reasonable care, bearing in mind the circumstances in which they are placed. In this case Basi was guilty of serious and dangerous foul play which showed a reckless disregard of the plaintiff's safety and fell far below standards which might reasonably be expected in anyone pursuing the game.

So, if you are a player, take care.

THE 'ESCAPE TO VICTORY' GAME

HUNGARY, JUNE–AUGUST 1980

John Huston's remake of the Hungarian film The Last Goal, released as Escape to Victory in Britain and Victory in the United States, was not well received by the critics. The film was more memorable for its soccer sequence than for its portrayal of the realism of war. (If only one could say that about all soccer games.)

Huston's film was set in World War Two. The match revolves around the idea that nations can settle their differences on the soccer field. A German commandant challenges a team of prisoners to a game against their German guards. Captain Colby, played by Michael Caine, organizes the prisoner-of-war team, which contains some very familiar faces. The actors are experienced professional footballers, like Brazilian Pele, Argentinian Ossie Ardiles, former England captain Bobby Moore and Scotland international John Wark. The team's goalkeeper, played by Sylvester Stallone, is more obviously a novice. During filming Stallone discovered that soccer was a very tough sport. Flinging himself around like an acrobat, Stallone broke a finger, damaged his knees and bruised other fingers. When he returned to the United States he described himself as a walking blood clot.

And so, to the climax of the film – the soccer game.

The Germans, to ensure a propaganda victory, have engaged the services of a supportive referee. At half-time the Germans have a 2–0 lead. Then comes a difficult decision for the prisoners. A tunnel has been dug to take them from their dressing-room to safety, but they also want to stay and see through the game – they feel they can win.

Sure enough, they continue the game rather than escape. They pull back the two goals and Stallone saves a penalty. The crowd invades the pitch and the team escape in the confusion.

Escape to Victory was not the first soccer film. The earliest talking picture to include soccer scenes was probably The Great Game, which staged a game at Barnes and included in its cast Jack Cock, an England international who was playing for Millwall at the time (1930). Later in the 1930s, the Arsenal Stadium Mystery was filmed from Leonard Gribble's book, and a few soccer sequences were set up to portray the fictitious crack amateur team called the Trojans. More recently, Sweden has produced Stubby, the United States has given the world Boys in Company C and The Longest Yard, while Britain chipped in with Yesterday's Hero and Gregory's Girl, the latter almost certainly being the pick of the lot.

Escape to Victory shows how a soccer game can be staged and filmed to suit an audience's fantasy or the director's concept of an unlikely encounter. There is, however, an element of truth in it. Soccer was indeed played in certain prison camps.

THE BROKEN GOALPOST

CHESTER, SEPTEMBER 1981

Plymouth Argyle's David Kemp headed the ball towards goal. Chester goalkeeper Grenville Millington stretched to make the save. He knocked the ball away and collided with an upright. The goalpost snapped near its base, the crossbar swung freely and the net caved in. Kemp thought he'd scored. Millington was too dazed to know.

That broken goalpost caused the first leg of the Chester– Plymouth first-round League Cup tie to be abandoned after 78 minutes. It became one of the few two-legged Cup ties to need a replay after the first leg. The score at the time was 2–2, Kemp having started the scoring, Steve Ludlam managing two for Chester and John Sims squaring the scores just a few minutes before the goal collapsed.

The teams met again at Chester the following week. The replay had one goal each in the first half, and they each had a goal to defend through the whole game . . . rather than just for 78 minutes. Another 1,700 spectators turned out (or was it the same 1,700 as the previous week?) but Chester had to fork out for a new goal and Plymouth bore the costs of another round-trip journey of over 500 miles.

A broken goal doesn't necessarily mean the end of a game. It depends how easily the damage can be repaired. There was a seven-minute delay at Wolverhampton in January 1957 and a 45-minute delay at Lincoln in August 1970. I'm not sure what that says about modern technology. At Lincoln they must have been tempted to muddle through as there were only a couple of minutes to play. Okay, lads, who's going to take off his shirt?

The 1957 incident at Wolverhampton is interesting for another reason. The opponents were Third Division Bournemouth, whose outside-left, Reg Cutler, ran into the netting, broke a goalpost, felt the net come down on top of him and lay tangled up like a caught fish. Cutler later scored the only goal of that fourth round FA Cup tie to provide one of the shocks of the 1950s.

It takes two goals to make a game, and broken goalposts can strike the biggest of clubs. In 1971, Borussia Moechengladbach, leading the West German Bundesliga, were playing at home to Werder Bremen. The score was 1–1 when the game was abandoned two minutes from time after a goal apparatus had collapsed. Borussia lost the game by default, as they were held responsible for not having a replacement goal, but they won the league anyway.

TEAM ON STRIKE

MAIDSTONE, JANUARY 1983

On New Year's Day, Weymouth were scheduled to play an Alliance Premier League game at Maidstone. Weymouth players were on a high, having won their last nine games, but the club was on a low, pondering an overdraft of £50,000 and losing £700 a week.

Ten players in the squad were based around Bournemouth, 35 miles from Weymouth. These players travelled to games and training by car. They were costing the club over £200 in expenses, and the club had another idea.

Weymouth directors calculated that hiring a mini-bus for Bournemouth-based players would help save £100 a week, but the players thought such a mid-season change would be in breach of their contracts. They sought advice from the Professional Footballers' Association and decided to strike.

On the morning of the Maidstone game the Weymouth team coach set off at 8.30 am. The driver was expecting to pick up the bulk of the squad at Ferndown, a few miles north of Bournemouth, a convenient meeting-place close to the main route east. Weymouth manager Stuart Morgan, Alliance Premier League manager of the month for December, was there. His Bournemouth-based players weren't. The coach had to turn round, and the game was postponed.

The strike lasted 48 hours. For a time it threatened the Monday home game with Bath City, Weymouth's tenth successive victory, and their third round FA Cup tie at Cambridge United, which resulted in a narrow 1–0 defeat.

The club reached a settlement by shelving the mini-bus idea and agreeing to go to arbitration. The Football Association mediated with an increase of £15 in Bournemouth-based players' weekly wages, in lieu of travel expenses. Almost all the players accepted this. The club had to face the consequences of failing to fulfil a fixture.

The Alliance Premier League fined Weymouth £100, ordered them to pay £895 to Maidstone for match expenses and losses and a further £182 towards the costs of the hearing. More controversially, Weymouth were docked 10 league points, taking them out of the Championship race.

By March, when Weymouth's appeal was heard by the Football Association, the Dorset club's season was heading downhill. They had won only one of their last six games, they had to face the possible loss of 10 league points and, at one away game, thieves had broken into their dressing-room during the game. A two-hour hearing at Lancaster Gate cleared the club of a charge of bringing the game into disrepute, ordered the fines and costs to stand, but, justifiably, agreed that the club should lose no league points. The FA offered the chance for three extra points, saying the match with Maidstone should be rearranged.

Maidstone won the game 3–0 but missed the Alliance Premier League Championship by a point. Weymouth ended their crazy season in seventh position.

THE 68-HOUR GAME

FLORIDA, AUGUST–SEPTEMBER 1984

When Ernie Schultz, a Miami student, left the field with exhaustion at 9.20 pm on 2 September 1984 it was hardly surprising. At that point the game between North Palm Beach Golden Bears and Palm Beach Piranhas had been going for 51½ hours.

The game eventually lasted 68 hours and 11 minutes, thus breaking the record for the longest-ever game. During this time one player broke an arm and there were several cases of exhaustion, Schultz being the first. The game was finally stopped when one team was down to only six fit players. The teams were following international rules whereby they couldn't continue with fewer than six on one side.

The game, which started on 31 August, was a systematic attempt at a world record for long play. The previous record (65 hours 1 minute) had been set by the Callinafercy club in Ireland four years previously. In the Florida game, the players averaged 19 years of age. They took five-minute breaks every hour and changed uniform 22 times.

There was a problem at the start. Someone forgot to tell the local police, and when local residents complained of the noise the game was ordered to another field six miles away.

'WE WANT TWENTY'

STIRLING, DECEMBER 1984

Stirling Albion had some trepidation about their first round Scottish Cup tie at home to Selkirk. The previous season Stirling were sitting on a huge lead at the top of the Scottish Second Division when they lost 2–1 at home to Inverness Caledonian of the Highland League, the winning goal coming in the last minute of extra-time. Stirling's season had gone downhill from there. They missed the chance of a Cup tie at home to Rangers, and they missed out on promotion. Stirling were still in the Second Division when they were drawn against Selkirk of the Border Amateur League W Division. The prevailing opinion, supported by Stirling manager Alex Smith, was that the game shouldn't be taken lightly. It wouldn't be easy.

Stirling sent chief scout George Rankin to watch Selkirk. He saw them take a 3–0 lead at Leithen Rovers and left before the finish. He didn't see them concede five in the last 20 minutes and go down to a 5–3 defeat.

Stirling Albion, meanwhile, were scoring four in the last 15 minutes of their match at Albion Rovers. Both sides, unwittingly, were warming up for their next week's Cup match, which would establish a British record for this century.

From the start to the end of the game, Stirling Albion showed no signs of underestimating their amateur opponents. Their five first-half goals were all scored by different players – Irvine (6 mins), Maxwell (12), Ormond (26), Thompson (34) and Dawson (36) – and Walker became the sixth Stirling player on the score-sheet shortly after half-time. Thereafter it was one long procession towards the Selkirk goal.

On another day, Selkirk goalkeeper Richard 'Midge' Taylor might have saved the 13th goal, and there was a suspicion of offside about the 19th, scored by Neil Watt. Otherwise, Stirling were pretty good value for their 20–0 win, and Taylor made some good saves to restrict the score to a score.

Stirling's second-half goalscoring was dominated by David Thompson, a £10,000 signing from Stenhousemuir, who scored six in the second half. The 20 goals were shared by eight players – David Thompson (7), Willie Irvine (5), Keith Walker (2), substitute Neil Watt (2), Scott Maxwell (1), Jimmy Ormond (1), Rab Dawson (1) and Gerry McTeague (1).

Selkirk player-manager Jackson Cockburn had the idea that his team might just be able to frustrate Stirling and catch them in the second half. There's no telling what would have happened had one of Selkirk's two shots gone in, or their one corner-kick had come to something. Towards the end, though, the dreams had been obliterated. I am reminded of a line in a report of Arbroath's 36–0 win over Bon Accord in 1885: 'After the 20th goal, Bon Accord played like a team with no hope.'

There was a touching moment near the end, when Stirling's score was in the high teens. Selkirk officials on the touch-lines collected as many numbers as they could and held them up to indicate they wanted to substitute them all. It was a pity there weren't more than a few hundred spectators present to laugh at the joke.

Stirling supporters, having chanted 'we want ten' after an hour's play, were able to chant 'we want twenty' in the last few minutes. At the end manager Smith thought his team had scored 19 rather than 20 goals. It was an excusable mistake. It was very easy to miss a goal.

This was Stirling Albion's second record of the 1980s. The other was not so positive. They failed to score a goal in the last 13 Scottish League games of 1980–1, altogether playing 1,293 minutes between McPhee's goal (31 January 1981) and Torrance's goal on the opening day of the next season (29 August 1981). That was probably the point at which they started saving them up for poor Selkirk.

Stirling Albion could justifiably be proud of their achievement of recording the biggest victory in British soccer this century, but Selkirk, completely outclassed on the day, could also be proud. Theirs had been an incredible achievement to reach the first round of the Scottish Cup for the first time.

A POOCH OF A GOAL

STOKE-ON-TRENT, NOVEMBER 1985

To say a dog scored a goal is understating the case. It's almost like saying England scored a fourth in the 1966 World Cup Final when a forward tapped in a pass from a defender. So let's give the dog full credit. This was no everyday goal by a dog. This was supreme opportunism at its best.

David Hall, secretary of Knave of Clubs, recalls the most amazing thing he has ever seen on a football field: 'We were playing Newcastle Town in the Staffordshire Sunday Cup, and 1 think we were losing 2–0 at the time. One of our players was running down the field with only the goalkeeper to beat. He tried a shot from 15 yards out and miscued it, so it was going well wide. The dog ran on to the field, jumped up at the ball and headed it. The ball flew into the net.'

The dog, a mongrel, disappeared before either secretary had a chance to sign him. He left behind an argument which will continue for years. Should the referee give a goal? David Hall explains: 'There was quite a crowd at Monks Neil Park. Most were laughing at it, but a lot didn't know what the rules would say. The Newcastle players argued that the referee couldn't allow a goal, but the referee did. Our side rejoiced, but their players weren't too happy.'

Newcastle Town hung on to win the Cup tie 3–2.

Like star midfield players, dogs can arrive from nowhere and make an impact on games. They are usually good at keeping their eyes on the ball and dribbling it, but not many are as good in the air as the mongrel at

Monks Neil Park. Unfortunately, for at least one footballer, dogs can also be strong tacklers. Chic Brodie was keeping goal for Brentford against Colchester in 1970 when a ferocious white mutt ran full pelt into him just as he was collecting a back-pass. The dog hit Brodie's left knee as he twisted and the goalkeeper suffered serious knee-ligament damage, enough to finish his career at Football League level. The nearest the goalkeepers' union came to exacting retribution on wildlife, as far as I'm aware, was a game in Holland. A high kick from the Feyenoord goalkeeper hit a pigeon which fell dead on to the field.

FIVE PENALTIES IN A GAME

LONDON, MARCH 1989

Referee Kelvin Morton, an accountant from Bury St Edmunds, helped create a new British record when he awarded five penalties in a Division Two game between Crystal Palace and Brighton and Hove Albion. All five came in a 27-minute period either side of half-time.

It was an extraordinary game. Palace's first goal, in the 23rd minute, was sparkling, Ian Wright hitting a volley some considerable distance from goal. When Brighton were reduced to ten men five minutes later – Mike Trusson was sent off for a foul on Eddie McGoldrick – Palace took complete control and earned three penalties in the space of five minutes just before half-time.

Mark Bright had taken over from Neil Redfearn as the Palace penalty-taker, and, in the last home match, he had scored with his first attempt. Bright's method used more power than subtlety. Against Brighton goalkeeper John Keeley he slammed in the first penalty to make the score 2–0, mishit the second penalty against Keeley's legs and opted not to take the third. Ian Wright obliged instead, and hit the ball against a post.

Six minutes after half-time Brighton themselves were granted a penalty – Alan Curbishley scored. Then Palace were awarded their fourth of the game. There was no shortage of willing takers. John Pemberton had a try. His shot went over the crossbar.

Brighton were considerably heartened by all this. Palace, on the other hand, having missed three penalties, still only 2–1 ahead, playing against ten men, worrying about their attempts to reach a Second Division play-off position, were growing agitated and nervous. A few more penalty misses might have inspired Brighton defenders to appeal for them in their own area while Palace players shouted 'Never, ref'. Brighton took advantage of Palace's loss of composure to make some late attacks, but Perry Suckling produced a couple of excellent saves and Crystal Palace hung on to win 2–1 when they should have won far more convincingly.

Prior to this Palace-Brighton game, there had been at least five games with four penalty-kicks – St Mirren–Rangers (1904), Burnley–Grimsby (1909), Crewe–Bradford (1924), Northampton–Hartlepool (1976) and Bristol City–Wolves (1977). In addition, other games with a concentration of penalties have certainly occurred outside Britain, including the Argentina–Mexico World Cup game in 1930 when five penalties (some disputed) were awarded. The Palace–Brighton game, on the other hand, aroused no real complaints about the referee's decisions. Palace manager Steve Coppell had only one misgiving – he felt his team should have scored with all four kicks rather than one. As a warning to them not to lose their composure again, he invited them back for extra training the day after the game.

A FLARE- UP FOR FIFA

RIO DE JANEIRO, SEPTEMBER 1989

The FIFA general secretary called it 'the biggest attempt at swindle in the history of FIFA'. It happened midway through the second half of a World Cup qualifying game between Brazil and Chile. Brazil led 1–0 at the time, and looked certain to qualify for the 1990 World Cup Finals. A draw was all Brazil needed, whereas Chile had to win.

Brazil had dominated the game to that point. Careca's goal, on the hour, was small reward for all the Brazilian pressure, but good goalkeeping by Roberto Rojas, the Chilean captain, had kept the lead to one. Rojas was also the principal actor in the drama which followed an incident in the 69th minute.

A 24-year-old Brazilian woman spectator threw a green signal-flare into the Chilean goalmouth while play was at the other end. It floated down, and a cloud of smoke appeared near the goalkeeper Rojas, who fell to the ground holding his face. Chilean players and medical officials gathered round the fallen goalkeeper, and, rather than wait for an official stretcher, they clumsily carried Rojas off the field. The goalkeeper appeared to be bleeding heavily from a cut on the face.

The rest of the Chilean team followed Rojas to the dressing-room. The Brazilian players stood around talking, and match officials waited. When spectators showed signs of impatience, troops were sent to the dressing-room to investigate. FIFA delegates soon joined them. Chile had decided to withdraw from the match, considering lives to be in danger, and the match therefore had to be abandoned. Thousands of the

160,000 spectators waited, many for as long as two hours, in hope that the game would be resumed.

The Chilean team doctor reported that Rojas had required five stitches in a facial cut, but the Brazilians claimed that the blood was simulated. Experts argued that signal-flares were harmless, whereas fireworks might cause such an injury. Photographs showed the flare had not hit Rojas and no blood was initially visible. A FIFA investigation confirmed the deception. Rojas admitted that he had faked his signal-flare injury.

FIFA suspended Rojas from national and international football for life. They also suspended several Chilean officials, including the team doctor, who had issued a false medical certificate, and the equipment official, who had disposed of the goalkeeper's gloves and jersey. Chile were banned from the 1994 World Cup Finals, while Brazilian authorities received a small fine for failing to make adequate security arrangements. Brazil were awarded a 2–0 forfeit victory.

History has shown that a team failing to complete a fixture is likely to be in serious trouble with the football authorities. Later that same month, September 1989, while the Brazil–Chile decision was still being settled, an English non-League team walked off the field. Dunstable Town player-manager Kevin Millett was incensed at a referee who sent off three of his team-mates during an FA Cup tie against Staines Town. He led off the remaining seven, and the tie was abandoned after 38 minutes.

FOOTBALL FOR PIGS

VARIOUS PIG FARMS IN BRITAIN, FROM JUNE 1990

While the world's football press concentrated on seemingly strange events, like Cameroon's defeat of World Cup holders Argentina, something was stirring at the grassroots of football. More and more pigs were taking up the game.

When Bernard Hoggarth visited the Paris Agricultural Show early in the year, he spotted a Danish product, the Domino Stress Ball, which enabled pigs to play football. Hoggarth bought some balls for his pig business at Cranswick Mill, near Driffield in Yorkshire, and, after successful trials, began marketing Stress Balls in Britain. The manufacturers claim that football-playing pigs are less aggressive and less stressed and therefore happier and more likely to put on weight. You may have heard the same argument applied to human footballers.

The product was publicized around the time of the 1990 World Cup Finals. There were suggestions that an international team of pigs should be managed by Franz Baconbauer, and an English Premier Cut League should include Trotterham Hotspur, Queen's Pork Rangers and Roast Ham United. It would appeal to those football-club groundsmen who claim they've seen dressing-rooms looking like pig-stys.

Pigs are intelligent creatures. When bored, they can become aggressive, and bite the tails or ears of other pigs in the pen. Hence the need to amuse them. Traditionally, some pig-keepers have suspended chains or left cans in pens to chew on. The Stress Ball is a more sophisticated toy. They roll it around the sty, shoot it into corners and leap over it on their way to their fodder,' says the promotion literature. In practice, pigs rely more on dribbling with their snouts than kicking the ball.

Stress Balls are indestructible. They are bright red, about eight or nine inches in diameter and made of sturdy plastic. Each one has a ball-bearing in the middle which rattles as the pigs knock the ball around the pen. A Stress Ball needs to be disinfected and cleaned after each batch of pigs, but can be used time and time again.

On his Yorkshire pig farm, Bernard Hoggarth experimented with one ball in a pen of about 15 pigs. The pigs tended to play with the ball on their own and when one had had enough another took over. No doubt this ability to pass the ball at the right moment can be developed further. Perhaps we will eventually see pigs playing team games, and spectators guaranteed lots of excitement around the pen areas.

It sounds like something out of Animal Farm, doesn't it? Those familiar with George Orwell's satirical fairy-tale may recall that the pigs learned to read, lead and stand on hind legs, and Animal Farm became a replica of the human society it had replaced. A manager of a soccer team of pigs would be especially vulnerable to the chop.

Stress Balls have also been supplied to breeding stables for racehorses to play with, but a well-hoofed shot could cause damage if it hits a passing spectator. At the time of going to press chickens had yet to be approached: the manufacturers were worried about too many fouls.

A RE-ENACTMENT GAME

BRADFORD, SEPTEMBER 1991
(AND THEN ANNUALLY ON CUP FINAL DAY)

On the night that Bradford City beat Newcastle United 3–2, supporters of the two clubs gathered in the Fountain Inn on Bradford's Heaton Road. The pub was the headquarters of the Heaton branch of the Bradford City Supporters Club and also of the Yorkshire branch of the Newcastle United Supporters Club.

'And we beat you in the 1911 Cup Final,' said one Bradford City fan.

'But that Cup Final goal was offside,' said a Newcastle fan.

Suddenly the conversation was more about the 1911 FA Cup Final than how that evening's result might affect City's changes of relegation or Newcastle's promotion aspirations. The Bradford City fans were aware of two recent events: a replica 1911 Cup Final shirt had been offered for sale; and the supporters club had been contacted by Richard Edwards of Coventry, who claimed to be a relative of Jimmy Speirs, scorer of the 1911 goal which gave Bradford City a 1–0 victory over Newcastle United.

Wouldn't it be a good idea to replay the 1911 FA Cup Final with a game between rival supporters?

The two sets of fans worked hard at arranging a re-enactment game, supported by the two clubs and the local newspaper. Bradford City offered the use of Valley Parade, but the date had to be changed from Tuesday 17 September to Sunday 29 September when a Rumbelows Cup game interfered. The Beamish Museum in County Durham helped to organise Newcastle United's replica kit, and special replica shirts were made for the Bradford lads. The 1911 ball was brought out of its showcase for publicity pictures and a replica programme was printed. On the day of the match, players sported period slicked-back hairstyles and false moustaches. The Newcastle United goalkeeper wore an authentic flat cap and City manager Philip Metcalfe dressed in bowler-hat and long coat.

The major beneficiary was the Burns Research Unit at Bradford University. It was just over six years since a tragic fire at Valley Parade had killed 55 people and injured 210 others. The programme sales for the re-enactment 1911 Cup Final raised £800.

Bradford City fan Mark Neale, the match organiser, later described the build-up in a special issue of the City Gent fanzine: 'In the dressing room, as the teams got changed we found ourselves the subject of much media attention as we dressed in the replica kits. Out on the pitch I was photographed from every angle holding the 1911 ball, and we really did not have time to savour the moment. As I went back into the dressing room, the teams were coming out at the request of the press for yet another photo. As a result we ended up on the pitch without any balls for the warm-up, without the match officials, and with me bursting to go to the loo! The rest, as they say, is history, although you could say that it's "recycled history" in this case.'

Neale and his team-mates were fulfilling a lifelong ambition of playing for City in a Cup Final at Valley Parade, although Neale would have preferred the game not to have started while he was still bursting for a pee. City mascot James Hodgkinson kicked off with the genuine 1911 ball. His great-grandfather Jimmy McDonald, Bradford City captain in 1911, would have kicked the same ball, which was quickly replaced by a modern equivalent.

Newcastle had the better of the first half and led 1–0 at the interval. The Bradford boys equalised in the second half. The game looked to be petering towards a 1–1 draw when the referee controversially awarded a late penalty to Newcastle. The penalty was converted and Newcastle won 2–1.

'It was never a penalty,' said the City lads after the game.

'We'll have to play it again.'

And so they have. The game is now played annually on Manningham Mills on the morning of FA Cup Final Day. The two sets of supporters continue to be friendly, and the bond was strengthened when professionals like John Hendrie and Peter Jackson played for both clubs. After each game, the two teams retire to the Fountain Inn to watch the Cup Final. The only exceptions, of course, come when Newcastle United reach the real FA Cup Final and the re-enactment match is delayed by a week.

Think of the fun the next time Bradford City and Newcastle United meet in the FA Cup Final.

PICKING THE WRONG PLAYERS

STUTTGART, LEEDS AND BARCELONA, SEPTEMBER AND OCTOBER 1992

'The manager picked the wrong players,' supporters moan when their team is knocked out of a Cup competition. Sometimes they are right. The most obvious example was the first round of the 1992–3 European Cup competition when VfB Stuttgart coach Uwe Hoeness indisputably picked the wrong players for the second leg of the tie against Leeds United.

Stuttgart won the home leg 3–0 and looked to be coasting in the return when Buck's 33rd-minute goal equalised an earlier effort by Gary Speed. Leeds continued to attack, however, and a Gary McAllister penalty just before half-time, a lob from Eric Cantona (60 minutes) and a Lee Chapman header from Gordon Strachan's corner (79 minutes) made the score 4–1 on the night. It set up an exciting last ten minutes but there were no further goals. The second leg ended with the scores level (4–4) and Stuttgart winners on the away goal.

Meanwhile, in Germany, alert television viewers had quickly spotted that it was Hoeness rather than Leeds manager Howard Wilkinson who had chosen the wrong players to do the job. The appearance of Adrian Knup and Jovo Simanic, two late substitutes, confirmed that the squad contained four foreign players when the maximum was three. The German television station showing the game was inundated with calls pointing out the mistake. The rule was broken when Hoeness named his squad: 'The 16 or fewer players chosen by a club to take part in any match under competition rules . . . should not include more than three players who are not eligible to play for the national association with which the club is registered.'

Clubs were given clear guidance as to what constituted a foreign player and what was an 'assimilated player'. The latter included players raised through a youth policy and players with five years at the club. Leeds United had three foreign players – Eric Cantona (France), Gary McAllister (Scotland) and Gordon Strachan (Scotland) – but Welshman Gary Speed was not considered foreign because he had been through the Leeds United training system.

The Stuttgart case was quite different. They quite clearly had four foreign players in the squad – Slobodan Dubajic (Serbia), Eyjolfur Sverrisson (Iceland), Adrian Knup (Switzerland) and Jovo Simanic (Serbia) – and the club admitted the mistake the day after the second leg at Elland Road. This was a very different case from the one that had occurred in Holland in the 1990–1 season. Feyenoord had then made a substitution which gave them three foreigners on the field during the game with Tilburg when the maximum permitted was two. The substitute was sent off and Feyenoord continued with ten men.

The Leeds-Stuttgart revelation caused a tricky problem for UEFA, who pondered over it for several days. Two options were available: disqualify Stuttgart from the competition and award the tie to Leeds United; or follow precedents and award Leeds a 3–0 home win. The four-man EUFA committee were split down the middle. After five hours of deliberation the two in favour of disqualification agreed to award a 3–0 win.

With the 3–0 home success the scores were level at 3–3 but Leeds United were still owed the chance of playing extra-time on their own ground. A 30-minute session at Elland Road would have constituted a really strange game, but instead the tie went to a replay on neutral ground. After mention of various locations – Basle, Berne and Rotterdam – the third leg of the tie was played at the Bernebeu Stadium, Barcelona.

On Friday 9 October a crowd of 10,000 rattled around the 120,000 stadium and watched as a late goal from substitute Carl Shutt brought Leeds a 2–1 victory. Shortly afterwards, though, Leeds were knocked out for a second time, beaten 4–2 on aggregate by Glasgow Rangers of Scotland in the second round.

'ONE TEAM IN TALLINN'

TALLINN, ESTONIA, OCTOBER 1996

Having beaten Latvia 2–0 in Riga on 5 October, the Scotland party flew to Tallinn in readiness for their next Group 4 World Cup qualifying match – against Estonia on 9 October.

The two countries had a good football relationship: Scottish fans had enjoyed visiting Estonia when the teams met in a 1993 World Cup qualifier and some of them had even returned to see the Estonia-Croatia game; Estonian officials had visited the Scottish Football Association to improve their understanding of football administration; and the SFA had sent equipment for Estonian youngsters. Yes, the two nations had a good rapport . . . until Scottish officials saw the floodlights in the Kadriorg Stadium.

In preparation for the 6.45pm kick-off, Estonian officials had arranged for temporary floodlighting to be brought from Finland. Scotland complained to FIFA that the low-level floodlights, mounted on lorries, would cause problems for goalkeepers when dealing with crosses from one particular side. It was reminiscent of floodlight debates in the fifties.

The next morning, at nine o'clock, FIFA announced that the time of the game would be changed from 6.45pm to 3pm. Scottish officials ran round all the locals haunts to spread news to their fans, buses were hired to ferry supporters to the ground and the players' preparations were changed accordingly. However, the Estonian officials pleaded that they had far more to consider – security arrangements in the stadium, consideration of supporters who were working during the day and the location of the players (80 kilometres from the ground). The most important thing, however, was the television contract, which had been arranged for a 6.45pm kick-off.

Scotland manager Craig Brown fully expected Estonia to conform with FIFA's ruling, so he went ahead with the preparations. Just before three o'clock John Collins led out Scotland but the opposition had still not arrived.

'One team in Tallinn,' sang the Scotland supporters. 'There's only one team in Tallinn.'

The Scotland players lined up for the kick-off. The referee, Miroslav Radoman of Yugoslavia, is probably the only referee in history who had to be certain that players couldn't be offside from a kick-off. (They must be inside their own half or the place-kick is retaken.) He blew the whistle and Billy Dodds tapped the ball to Collins.

The referee blew his whistle again.

The match was over.

Tosh McKinlay punched the air and raised his hands to the Scottish fans. Scotland thought they must have won the game by default as a FIFA directive stated that teams would win 3–0 if the opposition failed to turn up.

'Easy, easy, easy,' chanted the supporters.

No caps were awarded but the Scottish players were allowed to keep their shirts. They couldn't very well swap them with the opposition, could they?

As for the two teams:

ESTONIA:
SCOTLAND: Goram, McNamara, Boyd, Calderwood, McKinlay, Burley, Lambert, Collins, McGinlay, Dodds, Jackson.

The Estonia team bus arrived at the Kadriorg Stadium at five o'clock. They were too late for the game, such as it was.

On 7 November the World Cup organising committee met and decided that the Estonia-Scotland tie should be replayed on neutral ground. There was some disquiet about this decision, not least because the chair of the committee, Lennart Johansson, came from Sweden, and Sweden were in the same group as Scotland and Estonia. Scotland felt they (and their fans) were being punished for something that was no fault of their own. On 27 November it was announced that the re-match would take place in Monaco.

The next month the English Premier League had to deal with a similar situation when Middlesbrough failed to turn up for a match at Blackburn Rovers, claiming that 23 players were ill or injured. Middlesbrough were later deducted three points and fined £50,000, even though no formal directive seemed to exist. When that game was re-arranged, the two teams drew 0–0. The two lost points caused Middlesbrough to be relegated.

Estonia finally played Scotland on 4 February 1997. Scottish fans turned up with miners, glasses and special spectacles with torches to mock the floodlight farce in Tallinn. Scotland's only good spell came late in the first half. Duncan Ferguson's header was scrambled off the line, Tom Boyd's shot hit the crossbar, and Estonia goalkeeper Mart Poom made two wonderful saves. The match ended 0–0 but Scotland went on to qualify for France '98 as the best second-place finishers in the European groups.

Scotland kick off in Tallinn at 1.00pm to an empty stadium and more importantly an empty pitch. Three seconds later the referee blows to end the match, 9 October 1996. They were supposed to be playing a World Cup qualifier against Estonia but due to a disagreement over the kick-off time the home side failed to show up.

AS YOU WERE, LADS

CLEVEDON, SOMERSET, OCTOBER 1996

Witney Town and Clevedon Town were drawn together in a two-legged Dr Martens Cup first-round tie. The first leg was at Witney.

Adams scored for Witney in the 25th minute but a Jackson penalty levelled the scores. Witney had the better of the game but failed to get a winner. Indeed, only a last-minute save from Witney goalkeeper Alder saved the home side from defeat. The match ended 1–1.

'Clevedon's away goal could be crucial,' wrote Jon Adaway in the Oxford Mail. 'Witney must score in the second leg or face a quick exit.'

Later that same month Witney travelled to Clevedon for the second leg. The teams were again well-matched.

Adams scored for Witney in the 70th minute, but Winstone equalised eight minutes later. The second leg also finished 1–1. Extra-time followed.

In the 112th minute Winstone gave Clevedon the lead directly from a corner-kick but Crouch immediately equalised for Witney. The match ended 2–2 after extra-time.

The scores were level at the end of extra-time but Witney now had two away goals. At 10.05pm, the teams left the pitch and the spectators set off for home. Witney were through to the next round on away goals.

Or were they?

While the teams washed and dressed, the referee and the Clevedon Town secretary were speaking on the telephone to the secretary of the Dr Martens League. They all studied the rule-book and discussed the consequences. It appeared that away goals only counted double if they were scored in normal time. The correct ruling after 1–1 and 2–2 (after extra-time) was a penalty shoot-out.

Everybody back on the pitch.

Witney Town players were about to board their coach when officials went in with the bad news.

'You have to go back for a penalty shoot-out, lads.'

You can imagine how footballers would react to this.

'Come off it, Boss.'

'Pull the other one.'

Or words with similar meaning.

Eventually they realised that it was true. The players changed back into their dirty kit and went back out. A handful of spectators gathered behind one goal. One Witney official later described the whole scene as something akin to village football.

At 10.30pm a rather embarrassed referee began the penalty shoot-out. No doubt he would have sympathised with his counterpart in the 1895 FA Cup tie between Barnsley St Peters and Liverpool. Liverpool won that match 2–1 after extra-time only to learn later that the referee should not have played extra-time. The score was changed back to 1–1 and the teams replayed at Liverpool. Fortunately, Liverpool won the replay 4–0.

Fortunately again, for continuity's sake, Witney won the shoot-out 4–2 with successful shots by Caffel, Rouse, Phillips and Adams. Witney were now definitely through to the next round although the players found it hard to celebrate twice. They were also a little suspicious.

'Maybe it will go to a replay after all.'

But it didn't.

GOALKEEPER'S GOAL SAVES CARLISLE UNITED

CARLISLE, MAY 1999

'How long, Ref?' asked Carlisle United captain David Brightwell.

'Ten seconds,' the referee replied. 'This is your last chance.'

Carlisle United had won a corner-kick in the fourth minute of stoppage-time. They were drawing their match against Plymouth Argyle 1–1 but needed to win to preserve their Nationwide League Division Three status. All 11 players went up for the corner, including goalkeeper Jimmy Glass.

It had been a desperate week for Carlisle fans. On the Wednesday Scarborough had beaten Plymouth 3–0 to take their tally to 47 points, one more than Carlisle. It was the first time all season that Carlisle had been bottom of the table and the circumstances were ominous for the final Saturday. As Carlisle had scored only 41 goals to Scarborough's 49, it meant they had to win their last game at home to Plymouth to have any hope of saving themselves. The bottom club would be relegated, their place taken by Cheltenham Town, already promoted from the Nationwide Conference.

Scarborough drew their last match – 1–1 against Peterborough – and their fans celebrated when they heard that Carlisle were drawing in stoppage-time.

It was a tense game at Brunton Park, Carlisle, played in front of a 7,500 crowd. Plymouth had lost Paul Gibb with a broken leg, and had taken the lead just after half-time through Lee Phillips. Then David Brightwell had equalised superbly from 25 yards in the 62nd minute. And that seemed the end of the scoring . . . until the fourth minute of stoppage-time.

Goalkeeper Jimmy Glass, 25, had been signed on loan from Swindon Town in time to play the last three games of the season. Carlisle had been given special permission by the League to sign him after transferring goalkeeper Tony Caig and suffering further injuries after the transfer deadline. Scarborough later unsuccessfully contested the signing.

When it was obvious that the late corner-kick was Carlisle's last chance, the crowd behind Glass's goal shouted for him to get up the field. When manager Nigel Pearson waved Glass forward, the goalkeeper made a late run. Nearly a hundred yards.

The corner came across. Carlisle's Scott Dobie jumped in front of a defender and powered a header towards goal. Plymouth goalkeeper James Dungey parried the ball. And there was goalkeeper Glass, six yards out, still running. He met the loose ball with a crisp right-foot shot and scored.

Skipper David Brightwell saw the red goalkeeping shirt amidst the blue and green of the two teams and didn't realise at first that Glass had come up for the corner. He thought it was a fan on the pitch.

Suddenly Glass was lying on the floor under a crowd of players.

'I think I've just scored the winner,' Glass said.

In the Main Stand a blind Carlisle fan called David Ross heard his friend's commentary of the match give way to an almighty roar. But it was only later that Ross could comprehend that the goal had been scored by the goalkeeper.

Glass jogged back towards his own penalty area but the referee blew the final whistle immediately. Fans rushed on and Glass was chaired off the pitch.

'Four minutes into injury time, he saved a team in a way that no goalkeeper has ever saved anything before,' wrote Anthony Ferguson in the Carlisle News & Star.

On the Monday after the game Jimmy Glass handed over his size-ten boots so that a bronze sculpture could be made of them for display in the city's planned Millennium Gallery. Carlisle fans bought tee-shirts ('I believe in miracles') and other souvenirs of the incident. Meanwhile, Plymouth players could spend their summer thinking how best to mark goalkeepers from corner-kicks.

SENT-OFF PLAYER SUBSTITUTED

BIRKENHEAD, MERSEYSIDE, JANUARY 2000

First Division Tranmere Rovers were that season's Cup giant-killers. In the FA Cup fourth round, they led 1–0 against Premier League Sunderland, with two minutes of stoppage-time already played, when Clint Hill (Tranmere) fouled Alex Rae (Sunderland) in the Tranmere half. Hill was sent off by referee Rob Harris for a second cautionable offence. There was just enough time for Sunderland to launch a free-kick into the Tranmere penalty area.

In the dug-out area, the fourth official, David Unsworth, was dealing with the raging Hill, two managers (Peter Reid of Sunderland and John Aldridge of Tranmere Rovers) and two assistants (Adrian Heath and Kevin Sheedy). Before the Sunderland free-kick could be taken, Unsworth held up the board to signify a Tranmere substitution, but the board flashed the number six (Hill's number). Stephen Frail came on for Tranmere but nobody went off. Rovers still had 11 players on the field and Hill had been sent off.

Play resumed and the Sunderland free-kick was taken. A Sunderland player, under pressure from substitute Frail, headed the ball wide. Then the referee blew for full-time.

That left a quandary – should the match be replayed?

Starting with the Arsenal-Sheffield United replay, the authorities had had to make a number of difficult decisions about Cup-ties. An FA Cup second qualifying round tie between Herne Bay and Farnham had been replayed after Herne Bay used four substitutes instead of three in the original tie (September 1999). West Ham United had been told to replay a Worthington Cup quarter-final against Aston Villa for fielding an ineligible player (December 1999). One of the Hammers' substitutes, Manny Omoyinmi, who came on for the last eight minutes, had already played for Gillingham in the Worthington Cup earlier that season. West Ham lost the replay 3–1 after winning the first game (5–4 on penalties). Two staff members resigned over the Omoyinmi incident.

In the Tranmere-Sunderland case, the FA allowed the 1–0 result to stand. Sunderland manager Peter Reid had magnanimously credited Tranmere with winning the game 'fair and square'. Referee Rob Harris was suspended for two months.

Tranmere Rovers continued their FA Cup run by winning 2–1 at Fulham in the fifth round before losing 3–2 at home to Newcastle United in the sixth. That same season Rovers beat two Premiership teams – Coventry City and Middlesbrough – on the way to a Worthington Cup Final against Leicester City. Tranmere lost 2–1 to Leicester and Clint Hill was sent off again.

It was not long before Tranmere Rovers were involved in another strange match. In April 2003 they were leading Mansfield Town 2–0 only for the Division Two match to be abandoned at half-time. A fan had climbed on to the roof of a stand and refused to come down. Police decided to vacate the ground and, with the aid of the fire service, went on to the roof and helped the spectator down. The match was replayed two days later with Tranmere Rovers winning 3–1.

AUSTRALIA 31 AMERICAN SAMOA 0

COFF'S HARBOUR, AUSTRALIA, APRIL 2001

Having set a world record for a competitive international two days previously, by beating Tonga 22–0, the Australian national team went nine better against American Samoa in another Oceania World Cup qualifying group game.

American Samoa fielded a severely weakened team. Almost all of manager Tony Langkilde's original squad were ineligible because they did not have American passports, and most of his under-20 squad were unavailable as they were revising for examinations. Langkilde ended up with a young team (average age 19) which included one 15-year-old.

With a population of only 65,000 people, the American Samoa manager had a restricted choice anyway. In fact, FIFA rated American Samoa 203rd out of 203 countries.

At half-time the Australian Socceroos led 16–0 but were told to be professional in the second half. It was soon clear that American Samoa would suffer their record defeat, eclipsing the 18–0 loss in Tahiti the previous June, and their only hope would be for Australia to declare. American Samoa's only attack came in the 86th minute when Australia's goalkeeper Michael Petkovic saved a shot from Pati Feagiai. But Australia led 29–0 by then.

In a flurry of late scoring the scoreboard operator flashed up a 32–0 scoreline but the referee corrected him later. Archie Thompson scored thirteen goals, a world record for an international player. The previous record holders had been Sofus Nielsen (Denmark in 1908) and

Gottfried Fuchs (Germany in 1912) with ten in a match. Other than Australia, only Kuwait – against Bhutan in 2000 – have reached twenty goals in a match.

Australia went on to beat the winners of the other Oceanic Group (New Zealand) but lost 3–1 on aggregate to the fifth-placed South American team (Uruguay). Despite scoring 73 goals, Australia missed out on the 2004 World Cup Finals.

Teams like American Samoa have to start somewhere. Sark (population 550) is another small community that does well to field a team. In the 2003 Island Games, Sark lost to Gibraltar (19–0), Isle of Wight (20–0), Greenland (16–0) and Froya (15–0).

As the history of one-sided matches moves forward, so too does that of two-sided matches. This book already includes a match that ended 9–7 but that was replicated by Billington Synthonia's 9–7 win at Washington Nissan in the 2001–02 FA Carlsberg Vase. The match finished 6–6 after 90 minutes, and was poised at 8–7 before a last-minute goal by Ian Flanagan sealed the victory.

Another uncommon result was Weymouth's 8–5 win at Lewes in the FA Trophy in January 2004. Fans at the Lewes ground, known as the Dripping Pan, were spellbound as the goals kept going in. Weymouth led 3–2 after 20 minutes but Lewes equalised after 60 minutes. Then came seven more goals in the last half hour. Spectators debated among themselves how many Weymouth were ahead.

The Weymouth FC website put strangeness into perspective with the match report's final line: 'Incredibly this is not the first time Weymouth have won a match 8–5. The Terras recorded the same scoreline in a Dorset Senior Cup tie against Dorchester Town at the Rec on 3 December 1953.'

Anything can happen in football, and sometimes it can happen twice.

REFEREE SCORES WITH SUPERB VOLLEY

COLCHESTER, ESSEX, SEPTEMBER 2001

Put yourself in Brian Savill's place. You are refereeing a Colchester & District League match and Earls Colne Reserves are hammering Wimpole 18–1. You feel a little sorry for Wimpole.

It is a week after the terrorist attacks on New York City and Washington DC, and the mood is sombre. You are glad to be alive as you had a quadruple heart bypass operation almost exactly a year before. So you are looking for a way to celebrate life and cheer up everyone around you.

Then you see your chance.

Brian Savill's moment came ten minutes from the end of the game. A Wimpole player sent over a cross and the ball glanced off a defender towards the referee. Reacting on the spur of the moment, Savill raised his hand to stop the ball, then hit it sweetly on the volley with his left foot. The ball flew into the net and Savill awarded himself (and Wimpole) a goal.

There the fightback ended. The twelve men conceded two further goals and lost 20–2.

The incident was reminiscent of that created by dramatist Jack Rosenthal in a 1972 play called Another Sunday and Sweet FA. A referee is trying to control a match between two unruly local teams. He takes revenge by heading a goal for himself.

In Brian Savill's case, however, the critics were not amused. The Essex County Football Association charged him with bringing the game into disrepute and suspended him for seven weeks. Savill immediately ended his 18-year refereeing career by resigning. He was disappointed that his county FA couldn't see the funny side of the matter. In return the Essex FA were disappointed to receive the resignation. They couldn't afford to lose referees.

34 CONSECUTIVE SHOOT-OUT GOALS

HECKMONDWIKE, DECEMBER 2001

The penalty shoot-out system was introduced to ensure a winner, but there isn't always a winner. When Littletown played Storthes Hall, the players took 34 penalty-kicks before bad light stopped play at 17–17. Several months later the Guinness Book of Records confirmed that 34 consecutive goals in a shoot-out was a world record.

The two teams were from the West Riding County Amateur Football League. They met on 29 December in a first-round Premier Division League Cup tie. The score was 1–1 after 90 minutes, and extra-time brought no further goals.

Then came the procession.

'Next?'

'Well done.'

'Next?'

'Great shot.'

'Next.'

'Next.'

'Next.'

. . . until the score was 17–17 and one goalkeeper, Liam Garside (Storthes Hall), had scored twice.

Then failing light became a problem as there were no floodlights at the ground. Car-owners considerately switched on their headlights and the nearby street-lighting offered some help, but the ground eventually became so dark that one spectator described it as 'like playing down a pit'. The referee, Bob Hargreaves of Halifax, abandoned the match.

Only one question remained – how would they settle the tie?

Toss a coin?

More penalties?

A replay?

Straws?

Corner-kicks?

Golden goal?

Silver goal?

In fact, the match was replayed four weeks later.

Other penalty shoot-outs might have involved more kicks but not without a player missing. Indeed, it was more likely to find shoot-outs at the other end of the hit-miss spectrum. For instance, a Derby Community Cup tie in 1998 brought together two teams of children under the age of ten. The kids battled through a 66-penalty shoot-out before one team won 2–1. The first 60 kicks were missed. The children must have been exhausted.

A month before the Littletown-Storthes Hall contest, a new FA Cup record had been set when Macclesfield won a first-round replay by beating Forest Green Rovers 11–10 on penalties after a 24-penalty shoot-out. Curiously, three penalties had been awarded during regulation time, making 27 for the tie.

For sheer success, though, Littletown and Storthes Hall moved to the top of the list.

MATCH ABANDONED – TOO FEW PLAYERS

SHEFFIELD, MARCH 2002

The Nationwide Division One match between Sheffield United and West Bromwich Albion was abandoned after 82 minutes when Sheffield United were reduced to six men. This created an English precedent. In the past, matches had only been abandoned because of adverse weather conditions, pitch invasions, crowd disasters, stadium fires, fatalities or serious injuries on the field, and when dismissed players had failed to depart the pitch.

On several occasions teams had continued with fewer than seven men – for instance, Manchester City in 1906, Chelsea in 1931 – but these were before the International Board's decision on the matter. In living memory, the Football Association has followed the Board's recommendation that 'a match should not be considered valid if there were fewer than seven players in either of the teams'.

On 16 March, West Brom were third in Division One, and Sheffield United were fifteenth. In-form Albion were 11 points behind the second automatic promotion spot (with a game in hand) and this was a critical period.

Ill-feeling had spilled over from the previous season, managers Neil Warnock (United) and Gary Megson (Albion) had been at loggerheads, and the atmosphere was highly charged. Police and stewards were involved before the match when an Albion fan ran on to the pitch and baited United supporters.

In the eighth minute United goalkeeper Simon Tracey was sent off after handling the ball several yards outside his penalty area as Scott Dobie lifted the ball over his head. United replaced a striker, Peter Ndlovu, with their deputy goalkeeper, Wilko de Vogt. Dobie headed West Brom into the lead in the 18th minute, and their captain Derek McInnes added a superb second in the 62nd minute. A second Albion goal was strange in itself; 'one-nil to the Albion' was a contemporary catch-phrase.

With West Brom leading 2–0, Sheffield United manager Neil Warnock made two substitutions – Georges Santos for Michael Tonge and Patrick Suffo for Gus Uhlenbeek. The game immediately went out of control and both substitutes were sent off within minutes.

Santos renewed acquaintance with West Brom's midfielder Andy Johnson. A year previously Santos had spent five hours in surgery after fracturing a cheekbone in a collison with Johnson (then playing for Nottingham Forest). Now Santos made a terrible two-footed jump at Johnson. Santos was sent off and the injured Johnson had to be restrained by the physiotherapist and team-mates while still receiving treatment. Johnson limped off the field.

In the rumpus that followed, Suffo, the other substitute, headbutted McInnes with the referee nearby. Suffo was sent off, McInnes later had four stitches in the cut, and United were now down to eight.

Sheffield United captain Keith Curle, cautioned for a foul, then seemed to play as though he was seeking a second yellow card. But what stopped the match was two players departing the field with injuries.

By the time Michael Brown left the field, after 78 minutes, West Brom were 3–0 ahead, Dobie having added his second goal. Then Rob Ullathorne departed, and United's complement had fallen below the required seven. The referee, Eddie Wolstenholme, then made the correct decision to abandon the match after 82 minutes. His only alternative option was to call for a temporary suspension of play to see if one of United's injured players could return.

Derek McInnes refused to press criminal charges against Suffo when routinely asked by South Yorkshire Police. Five days after the match West Brom were awarded the three points. As Wolves had lost at home to lowly Grimsby Town, the momentum had swung towards West Brom, who went on to achieve automatic promotion.

Sheffield United later faced a number of charges from the Football Association. The club were fined £10,000 for failing to ensure that their players conducted themselves in an orderly manner. Manager Neil Warnock was cleared of a charge of improper conduct but he received a reprimand and £300 fine for his behaviour towards the fourth official. Suffo received a three-game suspension and £3,000 fine (on top of a three-match ban for the sending-off) and Santos would miss six matches altogether (four for the sending-off plus two more). Keith Curle received a two-match ban and £500 fine.

While Sheffield United-West Bromwich Albion was a precedent in English football, such abandonments had happened elsewhere, even in representative football: six Ecuador players were sent off in a 1977 international against Uruguay, and the match was abandoned at 1–1; the 2001 Angola-Portugal match was terminated when Angola were reduced to six (four sent off and one injured); five Rhodes players were sent off against Guernsey in the 2003 Island Games; and the 1992 Ethiopia-Morocco match in Rabat was abandoned after 65 minutes because the Ethiopians were down to six players. In the latter case, Ethiopia had had difficulty in fielding a team because six players had allegedly defected during an airport stopover in Italy. Ethiopia took the field with two goalkeepers in central defence and a 40-year-old coach in midfield.

In England, a 1999–2000 Worthington Cup tie between Millwall and Ipswich Town had been a close-run thing. Millwall had two players dismissed and then lost three to injuries after using all their permitted substitutions. On that occasion the referee consulted with the manager of six-man Millwall and an injured player was brought back on.

149 OWN-GOALS

TOAMASINA, MADAGASCAR, OCTOBER 2002

A scoreline of 149–0 looks like it belongs in a one-sided cricket match, but it also occurred when the Stade Olympique l'Emyrne (SOE) soccer team staged a protest by scoring 149 own-goals and losing 149–0 to AS Adema.

The SOE players were angry about a refereeing decision in their previous match, when they had conceded a last-kick equaliser to a disputed late penalty. That 2–2 draw, against Domoina Soavina Atsimondrano, meant that AS Adema had won the Championship. The final match was no longer a showdown between SOE and AS Adema with the title at stake.

The title was settled by a mini-league in which the top four teams played each other over an 11-day period. Before the final game, with the title decided, the SOE coach organised the protest. Everyone was amazed when his players passed the ball to each other from the kick-off and scored the first own-goal. On and on it went, own-goal after own-goal, until the referee did well to keep count. Angry spectators converged on the ticket-booths to demand refunds. One SOE central defender went on to score 69 own-goals, making him a real contender for the golden own-goal boot.

There have been games where three accidental own-goals have been scored in a match, but deliberate own-goals are very rare. It is possible that a player has scored an own-goal when trying to lose a match on purpose. It has also been suggested that a deliberate own-goal might act as an ethical solution to balance an unfair goal, such as Arsenal's second against Sheffield United in 1999. Dennis Evans (Arsenal) deliberately kicked the ball into his own net at the end of the 1955 match against Blackpool at Highbury, but only because he thought he had heard the full-time whistle and was celebrating a 4–0 victory. A few moments later Arsenal won 4–1.

Certain rules provoke players into planning own-goals. One example occurred in the Thailand-Indonesia Tiger Cup match of 1998. Both teams wished to finish second to avoid favourites Vietnam in the next round. With a few minutes left, the score at 2–2, Indonesia attacked their own goal. Despite fervent defence by Thailand, Indonesia's goalkeeper got hold of the ball and threw it into his own net. The authorities punished the teams involved.

An even stranger example occurred in the 1994 Shell Caribbean Cup. The rules stipulated that drawn group matches would be decided by Golden Goals. More interestingly, an extra-time winning goal would count double in the for-and-against columns.

In the preliminary round, Group 1 consisted of Barbados, Puerto Rico and Grenada. Puerto Rico beat Barbados 1–0 on 23 January, and two days later Grenada beat Puerto Rico 1–0 with a Golden Goal which counted double.

When Barbados met Grenada on 27 January, Barbados had to beat Grenada by at least two goals to win the group and qualify for the next round. Barbados led 2–0 until the 83rd minute when Grenada scored a crucial goal. Then, with a few minutes to play, Barbados realised that they could score an own-goal to take the match into sudden-death overtime, and then score a proper goal which would count double. After scoring an own-goal, however, they had an awkward few minutes while defending at both ends of the pitch. A goal at either end would have taken Grenada through.

In overtime, Barbados won the game 3–2 and as this counted as 4–2 they pipped Grenada on goal difference. So Barbados went through after scoring a deliberate own-goal.

A GAME OF 25 HALVES

READING, SEPTEMBER 2004

In a game of twenty-five halves Trevor McDonald's XI beat the Elstead Village Idiots by a cricket score – 197 to 69 – and it needed a cricket scorer to keep count. On the sidelines Mary Clotworthy kept a tally of the goals and goalscorers.

The match kicked off at 1pm on Saturday 25 September and ended at 2 pm the following day. During those 25 hours the players developed a routine of playing a 45-minute 'half' and then resting for 15 minutes. The breaks weren't so much half-time intervals as four-percentile respites.

The venue was the Clayfield Copse Recreation ground in Caversham Park Road. The players aimed to raise money for Comic Relief while posting a Guinness Book of Records benchmark for the longest-ever football match. The 25 players ranged in age from fourteen to forty-two. To qualify for the marathon they needed a doctor's certificate to prove their fitness. First-aid was present at the ground, and lots of water for the players to drink. The floodlights were switched on during the hours of darkness.

There were three injuries during the match so resources were stretched. One player had to continue for eleven hours. Others did their best to get some sleep on the sidelines while the match went on and on and on and on. By the end some players could hardly walk. Afterwards organizer Daniel Lewis claimed that he was planning to set another record – for the longest-ever sleep.

'DODGY LASAGNE'

LONDON, MAY 2006

The term 'dodgy lasagne' entered football folklore after the last day of the 2005-06 Premiership season. Tottenham Hotspur's final match was at West Ham United. A win would guarantee Spurs fourth place, a spot they had held since December, and qualification for the UEFA Champions League. Fifth-place Arsenal wanted to win their last match, at home to Wigan Athletic, and hope for a Spurs slip-up.

A party of over twenty Spurs players were booked into the five-star Marriott Hotel in east London. The players arrived at 7pm and soon afterwards enjoyed a buffet supper in one of the hotel's private rooms. The Spurs nutritionist had been consulted on the content of the meal and all seemed well until the early hours of the morning. Then a number of players were taken ill. At 5am Spurs manager Martin Jol was woken up by a phone call from the club doctor saying that seven of his players had upset stomachs. No other hotel guests seemed affected.

At 11.15am a Spurs official talked to the hotel general manager. The police were called in, and Tower Hamlets council's health and safety department was informed. About twenty police officers arrived around 12.30pm and forensic scientists took away samples of food. By now lots of rumours were spreading around the city. The chief rumour was that the ill players had all eaten lasagne from the buffet. Some informants said that not all the ill players had eaten lasagne. Reporters identified a whole smorgasbord of food available in the Spurs buffet – pasta, salad, chicken, steak and so on.

At noon Spurs requested a postponement or a delayed kick-off in order to allow the players more time to recover. The Premier League said 'No' to a postponement as Spurs clearly had enough fit players on the books to fulfil the fixture and could up replacements for such a local fixture. The police were against any extended delay because soccer fans were already drinking in pubs and too much drinking time was dangerous. A two-hour delay was offered but Spurs officials felt the players needed more time than that to recover. Tottenham officials knew that failing to fulfil the fixture would have serious consequences – Middlesbrough had been deducted three points in 1996-97 for failing to play at Blackburn and the punishment had ultimately cost the club relegation – so at 1.25pm everyone agreed that the match would start on time. Police accompanied the Spurs players on the journey to the stadium.

It was one of Tottenham's worst performances of the season. A number of players looked below par and illness offered an obvious explanation. Carl Fletcher gave West Ham a ninth-minute lead but Jermain Defoe equalized before half-time. Meanwhile Arsenal had gone 2-1 behind to Wigan before levelling at 2-2 by half-time. If both matches stayed level then Spurs would keep fourth place.

Spurs goalkeeper Paul Robinson kept Spurs in the game by saving a penalty kick by West Ham's Teddy Sheringham early in the second half. After Arsenal had taken the lead against Wigan Yossi Benayoun scored a late winner for West Ham. Arsenal went on to win 4-2, Spurs lost 2-1, and Arsenal took the last Champions League place. And it was all down to a 'dodgy lasagne'.

Or was it?

In fact the Health Protection Agency and Tower Hamlets Council environmental officers eventually agreed that food poisoning was not the likely explanation. The probable cause was an outbreak of a form of gastro-enteritis called norovirus. Tests on the players showed that one player had a form of gastro-enteritis that could have spread to the other players. The Marriott Hotel was thus exonerated.

In the ten days before the test results materialized the rumour grew stronger. The term 'dodgy lasagne' entered football vocabulary as a symbol of something that goes wrong with preparations and affects the participants. In the way that the expression 'sick as a parrot' gives parrots an unfair reputation – some species of parrot can outlive humans – so does 'dodgy lasagne' give the hotel business a bad name. But conspiracy theories live on to this day.

THE MATCH IN THE RIVER

BOURTON-ON-THE-WATER, GLOUCESTERSHIRE, AUGUST 2007

Footballers wade crab-style through six inches of water as they chase the ball towards the riverbank, kicking up spray and splashing spectators in the front rows. A player flicks the ball out of the water with his foot and volleys it upstream. The men wrestle with each other as they set off again.

This is the annual football match in the river at Bourton-on-the-Water, a town known as 'the Venice of the Cotswolds'. The River Windrush runs through the centre of Bourton-on-the-Water. Normally the river bubbles like a tame stream but in July 2007 it burst its banks. The High Street green turned into a lake and a hundred homes and businesses were flooded. Bourton-on-the-Water became 'Bourton-in-the-Water' or 'Bourton-under-Water'.

In the context of Gloucestershire's biggest-ever peacetime emergency – 48,000 homes lost electricity for two days, and about 350,000 people in the county were without mains drinking water for much longer – it was amazing that a match was played in the River Windrush five weeks after the floods. But the Bourton-on-the-Water river football match is one of Gloucestershire's great traditions – others include cheese rolling and woolsack racing – and the show must go on.

The players were mostly from Bourton Rovers, a Gloucestershire Northern Senior League team. The 'pitch' for the 2007 match was set up between the two bridges in the town centre. In the game's early days the bridges acted as goalframes. In modern times portable goals are put in the river in front of the bridges.

Nearly a hundred people congregated on each bridge. Those at the front dangled their legs off the edge. Hundreds of other spectators lined the riverbanks to watch the big match and some hung out of the windows of nearby houses. Children paddled in the water directly behind the goals. It was Bourton Rovers' largest attendance of the season and collectors went round with buckets.

The referee started the 2007 match by kicking the ball up in the air and the raucous scene was under way. Players were soon deliberately splashing each other and jostling like kids in a swimming pool. When one player did an orchestrated belly-flop in front of the referee he was shown a yellow card for diving. He wasn't the first person to have dived in a river.

Regular spectators in the front row of the riverbank knew to wear waterproof clothing and carry umbrellas. Others screamed and shrieked when hit by a spray of water. Tourists captured the scene with their cameras. Players shouted instructions to each other and a lot of energetic water fights took place away from the ball. The goals fell over a couple of times.

A wild clearance sent the ball into the crowd.

'Keep the ball in the river.'

The goalposts were so close to the riverbank that it was relatively easy to send the ball into the goalmouth from a throw-in. Players from both teams lurked in front of the smaller-than-normal goals as the ball looped through the air. Heading the ball was a relief after trying to kick it.

The rules of the Bourton match are not dissimilar to those of swamp soccer, a sport played on a pitch that has been rotavated and then soaked with hundreds of gallons of water. Swamp soccer and river football are both six-a-side games that rely on determination, energy and strength rather than raw football talent. In both codes the players take penalty-kicks and free-kicks by dropping the ball from their hands on to a favoured foot. Whereas the Bourton river game began in 1894, the year Bourton Rovers were founded, swamp soccer has a much shorter history, starting in 1997 when a group of cross-country skiers in Finland discovered playing soccer in a swamp was a fun way of building up leg muscles in training. Also, the names of swamp-soccer teams are more inventive. The swamp-soccer World Championship features teams such as Real Mudrid, Cowdungbeath, Inter the Mud and Dirt Kuyt FC.

Water matches take a heavy physical toll. A thirty-minute match in the River Windrush leaves players' feet feeling like ice, even on a hot August day. Players will tell you that 30 minutes of playing in the river is harder than 90 minutes on land. And swapping shirts is physically challenging. Getting them off your back is hard work. Then comes the wringing out.

In 2007, in the River Windrush, the Reds missed a penalty-kick but beat the Whites 2-1 before celebrating wildly and wetly with a sing-song in the river. The following year the riverbanks were strengthened against the possibility of further flood.

A large crowd watches the annual Whit Monday Football Match in the River Windrush between the bridges at Bourton-on-the-Water, Gloucestershire, June 1955.